Dogged Pursuit

Dogged Pursuit

My Year of Competing Dusty, the World's Least Likely Agility Dog

ROBERT RODI

HUDSON
STREET
PRESS

HUDSON STREET PRESS
Published by the Penguin Group
Penguin Group (USA) Inc., 375 Hudson Street, New York, New York 10014, U.S.A. • Penguin
Group (Canada), 90 Eglinton Avenue East, Suite 700, Toronto, Ontario, Canada M4P 2Y3 (a division
of Pearson Penguin Canada Inc.) • Penguin Books Ltd., 80 Strand, London WC2R 0RL, England •
Penguin Ireland, 25 St. Stephen's Green, Dublin 2, Ireland (a division of Penguin Books Ltd.) •
Penguin Group (Australia), 250 Camberwell Road, Camberwell, Victoria 3124, Australia (a division
of Pearson Australia Group Pty. Ltd.) • Penguin Books India Pvt. Ltd., 11 Community Centre,
Panchsheel Park, New Delhi – 110 017, India • Penguin Group (NZ), 67 Apollo Drive, Rosedale,
North Shore 0632, New Zealand (a division of Pearson New Zealand Ltd.) • Penguin Books (South
Africa) (Pty.) Ltd., 24 Sturdee Avenue, Rosebank, Johannesburg 2196, South Africa

Penguin Books Ltd., Registered Offices: 80 Strand, London WC2R 0RL, England

First published by Hudson Street Press, a member of Penguin Group (USA) Inc.

Excerpt from "Friendless," music by Benny Carter and lyrics by Paul Vandervoort II.
Reprinted by permission of Bee Cee Music Company.

REGISTERED TRADEMARK—MARCA REGISTRADA
HUDSON
STREET
PRESS

ISBN 978-1-59463-054-5

Printed in the United States of America
Set in Perpetua

For Haven Kimmel

CONTENTS

Contents

Tragically, Hip

C armen plunged through the suspended tire.

She sailed over a pair of jumps.

She scampered up the teeter, and when it swiveled on its axis and bit the earth, scampered back down again.

She took another jump, like an economy-sized gazelle.

She braided herself through the weave poles with virtuoso ease.

And then we arrived at the end of the course: just one final jump, no problem for my girl. She could clear it in her sleep.

"Over!" I commanded.

She galloped toward the bar, the wind in her ruff and a smile on her lips.

But at the last conceivable moment, she banked and went around the jump instead of over it.

Before I could bring her back to try again, she was past the finish line and out the gate, which meant she hadn't qualified. "NQ'd," as we say.

I forced myself to clap my hands and say, "Who's my athlete? Who's my rock star?" and give her back a good rubbing, because in the field of canine agility it is never permissible to show anger or frustration. The philosophy is: when your dog screws up it's your fault, not hers. So even after a disastrous run, you're still meant to be upbeat and say what a fantastic little trooper she is, and who wants a biscuit then?

I couldn't understand why she'd deliberately blown a jump. She liked agility. She enjoyed competing. Hell, we hadn't even been at it very long—it still had novelty value.

In fact only a year before, at a dinner party, I'd found myself bemoaning the difficulties of raising a fiendishly intelligent, demoniacally driven Shetland sheepdog. My partner and I had just moved into a big Victorian house nestled on a city block between two apartment buildings, with a large backyard that seemed to cry out for a canine to complete it. But once we'd installed her there, we began to realize she required more than just real estate.

"We're basically sedentary," I said to Sally, a longtime friend seated across the table from me. "Two middle-aged men who spend all their spare time staring at a computer screen. It drives the dog crazy. Then when we take her out for a walk, she goes berserk; everything overstimulates her. Maybe we're selfish to have adopted her at all. Is it cruel to keep a herding dog in a city of two and a half million people?"

Sally apparently had strong opinions on the subject, because she jabbed the air with her salad fork to hold my attention while she swallowed a bit of frisée, then gasped out, "She needs something to do; she needs a *job* to keep her happy."

The notion surprised me. Jeffrey had a corporate career that demanded long hours; and while I worked from home that still meant, well, *work*. I suppose we thought at least one member of the household would be glad to lead a life of leisure. Maybe the two of us, enslaved to our professional duties, had wanted to live vicariously through Carmen as she dozed the day away under the maple tree or basked in the sun on the deck.

But Sally wasn't having it. "No no," she said, "these are *working* dogs. They aren't happy unless they've got tasks, chores, something to challenge them."

For the life of me, I couldn't imagine what she meant. What "tasks" could I possibly assign Carmen? Our only current need was for a little light bookkeeping, and I doubted this was within her skill set.

"You aren't suggesting I go out in the yard and throw a ball for her, are you?" I asked, aghast. Nothing would be more likely to sap my will to live. And I couldn't imagine Carmen finding it any more felicitous.

Sally briskly shook her head, and then she mentioned canine agility. I'd never heard of it and asked what she was talking about.

"Doggie track and field, basically There's an obstacle course, and the dog has to run it. With you alongside, telling her what to do next."

"What kind of obstacles?"

"Bar jumps, hoop tunnels, a teeter-totter—that kind of thing."

This sounded at least minimally diverting. "They have this in the city?"

"You can train for it here, sure. I did it for a while with Pierre"—her late border collie. "And if you get good at it, you can compete in trials, though those are usually way out in the country."

"Oh, we don't want to get fanatical," I said, somewhat appalled at the idea of actual competition. I had the typical urbanite's disdain for people who became too deeply enmeshed in their leisure-time activities—who, for instance, frequent *Star Wars* conventions or play golf. "But giving her a good workout a couple times a month? That sounds ideal. Where can we do this?" Sally directed us to a doggie day-care facility on Chicago's Near North Side, which boasted a large training room and a full complement of equipment.

I was intrigued, certainly, but I had a nagging fear that the activity might turn out to be terribly adorable. I spent the next morning researching it online, visiting agility Web sites and even watching some videos of agility dogs in action. To my relief, the cute factor was nonexistent. This was a real sport, and these animals were fierce competitors. As, it seemed, were the human "handlers," who showed equal focus and drive as they ushered their dogs through the obstacles to a triumphant dash past the finish line. This was, beyond doubt, the only sport I'd yet seen in which one member of the winning team congratulated the other by licking his face.

So I called the day-care facility. As luck would have it, a new session was beginning that very Thursday. And since Jeffrey was out of town on business, I undertook Carmen's training on my own.

Thus once a week, in a class with a dozen other students, I found myself learning from a wisecracking, charismatic instructor named Dee how to maneuver the "obstacles" employed in agility:

the bar jump, the A-frame, the suspended tire, the dog walk (known anywhere else as a catwalk), the teeter, the tunnel, the chute, and the weave poles.

Soon Carmen had perfected her way over, under, or through all these, and we progressed to the next level of training, in which the obstacles were arranged to form a specific course. I, as her handler, learned to guide her through it—off leash, using only voice commands and gestures—the object being to tackle the obstacles in the prescribed order, with a focus on accuracy and speed.

Carmen seemed to thrive and became more enthusiastic even as the courses grew longer and more difficult. And as our grasp of these new complexities increased, so did my ambition. Inevitably, the once-a-week class led to an occasional weekend adventure. In other words, we crossed the Rubicon and went pro, traveling to agility trials around the Midwest and competing against other dogs and handlers. Not that we were *like* them, though: we weren't fanatics. We were just out for some kicks.

Carmen did well, earning a few novice titles and a fair number of first-place ribbons. Then she began to quail a bit, balking before obstacles in a manner that officially constituted "refusals," and earned deductions from the total score.

And finally, today, she deliberately evaded a jump.

I wondered if she was feeling all right. She wasn't yet a senior dog—she was only five—but purebreds are unfortunately prone to certain physical defects and ailments. So I took her to our vet, and sure enough she was diagnosed with canine hip dysplasia, a degenerative condition. While the problem wasn't especially serious—her insouciant demeanor hadn't been affected—it seemed clear her agility career was over. I couldn't in good conscience put her in the ring and demand that she do things that caused her pain.

And so, after a brief but valiant career, she was sidelined. Her box of ribbons would never brim over. I installed weave poles in the backyard so that I could still put her gently through her paces every now and then and treat her like a gold medalist afterward. With luck, she wouldn't miss agility at all.

And yet, paradoxically, I found *myself* missing it. The weekends on the circuit, which so alarmed me when I first heard about them, had become something I actually liked. Liked a lot. Needed, even. Not in a crackhead way, or anything. It's just that agility had proven to be more than merely a way of providing work for working dogs. It was very much a matter of collaboration, a meeting of minds. I lamented that I would never experience that kind of intense rapport again.

But then I realized I could. Not only that, I could return to agility with real purpose this time: no longer to dabble but to see how far I could go—to what lengths the peculiar alchemy of handler and hound could take me. To find out whether that strange, seemingly psychic bond could translate into real, quantifiable achievement; whether it could lead to mastery—to *championship*.

And all I'd have to do was get another dog.

Part One

CHAPTER 1

To Dusty I Shall Return

I decided to stick with Shelties, because their diminutiveness, intelligence, and drive make them ideal agility competitors. (Also, excuse me, but gorgeous much?)

I also decided my new Sheltie would be a rescue dog. I admired the work the various breed-based rescue societies were doing—seeking out orphaned, abandoned, and abused purebreds, housing them in foster homes, rehabilitating them if necessary, then endeavoring to place them with responsible new owners—and the surest way of showing my support would be to adopt one of their foundlings.

Like most such groups, Central Illinois Sheltie Rescue has its own Web site, to which I became a frequent visitor. The home page features photos of the available dogs, accompanied by descriptions of their ages, histories, and temperaments as well as a slug line denoting their adoption status. When I first visited, most of the photos revealed the kind of Shelties you'd expect: shameless charmers, working the camera, bright eyed and smiling, and just exuding gleeful positivity. Game-show hosts with fur. There was one, however, who broke the mold; Dusty was his name—presumably after his charcoal and ash coloring—and he looked, well, funny. In both senses of the word. His coat was thin and limp, not the usual luxurious Sheltie ruff that resembles the high-collared stoles worn by 1930s screen queens. And though the description praised his "long, elegant nose," it looked distinctly anteaterish to me. His eyes were too big, nearly marsupial. And given that his limbs appeared to be made of pipe cleaner, the general impression was one of wiry, anxious misanthropy. If Iggy Pop were a dog, this is how he'd look. In fact when I first glanced at Dusty's photo, the phrase that came to mind was "heroin chic." A moment later I changed my mind and dropped the "chic."

His status was listed as "available," which wasn't much of a surprise. The accompanying text did mention that he'd make a good agility dog because he ran very fast and could jump a five-foot fence, but I had to wonder how they came to discover this. And how far they'd had to chase him once they'd learned it. He had a definite look of prison break about him, and what I wanted was the traditional Sheltie eagerness to please—the trembling, expectant look that said: "Anything you want—just name it. I'll do it *right now*! Hey, are you *listening*?!"

When I returned to the site a few weeks later, Dusty was still there, but his status was now listed as "adoption pending." I was glad for him and had a momentary vision of him fitting perfectly into some *Addams Family*–type environment, where his close resemblance to a bat would be just the thing.

There were a few new dogs, including a gorgeous sable, Stormy, so named because he'd been found wandering the streets in the midst of a downpour. I'm a sucker for that kind of thing: a good, visually evocative story. And the temptation to enter such a story and become its hero—to give it the ending it deserves—can be overwhelming to someone of my sensibility. "And so our rain-drenched stray finds happiness and fulfillment in a loving Queen Anne home with weave poles in the backyard." Before I knew it, I was batting out an e-mail: "Hi, I would like to adopt Stormy."

It was several days before I saw a reply, and when Natalie, Stormy's foster mom, finally did get back to me, she had disappointing news: he'd been adopted in the interim.

I was astonished. How had this happened so quickly? Just a few days before Stormy's listing still read "available." "Actually," Natalie replied, "a couple came up to adopt one of the other dogs and fell in love with Stormy instead."

By this time I'd gone back to the site and, sure enough, Stormy had been removed from the roster. But Dusty was still there—*his* status downgraded back to "available." I asked Natalie whether the people who adopted Stormy had originally been interested in Dusty.

"Exactly so," she e-mailed back, a hint of resignation seeping from between the lines. "And it's not the first time either. Just last month someone came up for Dusty and ended up going home with another dog."

I felt my throat start to constrict—the onset of an emotional investment. Here was a narrative that badly needed a happy ending. I could take this scrawny, scruffy, unsmiling little beast away from his life of unremitting rejection and set him up in fully rehabbed Victorian splendor.

But I also wanted to train a champion, to get back into the agility ring, to go all the way to the top. I wanted ribbons, titles, *glory*. The desire was so strong, I could actually taste it on the back of my tongue—dark, smoky, and persistent.

So there I was, torn by conflicting imperatives. The amateur athlete in me insisted on a conventional, ballsy, go-for-the-gold Sheltie. But the yarn spinner in me wanted to take charge of *this* dog's story—to give it the kind of climax that would make readers weep and audiences cheer. What was I to do?

I looked back at the Web page. Well, it did say Dusty had agility potential. That seemed to split the difference. I shot back an e-mail saying—as noncommittally as possible—that I'd be willing to have a look at him.

It wasn't as simple as that, I soon learned. With all the paperwork I filled out, I may as well have been adopting a Romanian baby. And then I had to be (excuse the pun) vetted. A pair of Sheltie-rescue volunteers came out to give me a good looking-over, all but checking my teeth and fondling my fetlocks. They inspected the house and finally met Carmen, who gave her best wiggling-bottom welcome and enthusiastically agreed to put on a weave-pole demonstration.

Two days later I got the news: I'd been approved and could arrange a date to drive out and meet Dusty. At this point I was still telling myself that I didn't have to adopt him. This was an exploratory errand only. No one could force me to take him. I was an American citizen, a taxpayer, and a college graduate, and I knew my rights. I don't carry a gun, but I know several lawyers and can dial a mean cell phone when cornered.

It was only after I'd made the date and was mapping my route that I realized that paying a call on Central Illinois Sheltie Rescue would involve actually driving to central Illinois. In fact I would be going to Bloomington, a good two hours plus from my home in the heart of Chicago—an awfully long trek for someone who wasn't 100 percent convinced there was something waiting for him at the other end. But I reminded myself that once I'd gotten seriously into agility, I'd be doing a whole lot of long-distance driving. So I should just gird my loins, square my jaw, and start getting used to it now.

Eventually, after an endless, enervating succession of highways, strip malls, and industrial parks, I arrived at Natalie's house, tucked away in a placid, sunny little development like you'd see in a 1960s sitcom. It couldn't possibly have been more white-bread. I'm half Italian, half Irish, yet suddenly I felt wildly ethnic. I rang the doorbell and heard a chorus of affronted barking, so there was no question that this was the right house.

Natalie answered the door. She was a pleasant-looking woman in a pastel Sheltie sweatshirt, with a quantity of blond hair styled in a way I haven't seen outside of John Waters movies. I tried not to stare, but I was fascinated, as though I'd suddenly descended on Laplanders in native dress. Her husband appeared behind her; he was barefoot, which I took as an indication that we would not be standing on ceremony.

I was eager to get a look at Dusty—whose voice I presumed was one of those still yapping furiously a few rooms away—but first I was obliged to sit at the kitchen table (piled high with canine staples and accessories) and go through the contract, clause by clause. I was beginning to wonder whether it might in fact have been easier to just get that Romanian baby. Though I had my doubts about how well a little Constantine or Irina would maneuver the weave poles.

"Well, I guess that's it," said Natalie as we came to the end of the last page. "Are you ready to meet Dusty?"

"Darn tootin'!" I said. Being in the suburbs was clearly taking a toll on my speech patterns.

Natalie's husband opened an adjacent door, and a half-dozen Shelties tumbled in as though they'd all been listening with their ears pressed against it. They quickly righted themselves and started barking, circling each other, circling me, barking some more, and generally calling attention to themselves in the most intimidating manner possible, which, given that they were Shelties, wasn't very intimidating at all.

They were handsome specimens with bright eyes and bouncing coats. All but one. And when I saw him, my heart sank. When he spotted me, he reacted no better. He stopped short, backed carefully away, and took up refuge under a chair, from the shelter of which he glared out at me balefully. His pipe-cleaner limbs were poised to attack should I be reckless enough to approach.

"That would be Dusty," said Natalie, but I'd already inferred as much; who else could he be? A mutant horsefly, maybe, that slipped in while the door was open? To my surprise he was much scrawnier and odder looking than the photo had led me to believe. Was there an *Extreme Makeover: Canine Edition* they'd sent him to just prior taking his picture?

Natalie's husband fetched some American cheese slices from the refrigerator and handed them to me. "Offer him some," he said. "Make him come to you."

"He likes cheese?"

"All dogs like cheese," he said confidently, as though it were a maxim.

I tore away a quarter of one of the slices and dangled it toward Dusty. "Cheese!" I said. "Mmm, yummy! *Cheese*, boy! Hubba hubba!"

Immediately, I was accosted by five other Shelties, all prancing and dancing on their hind legs and doing whatever else they could to prove that "I deserve it, over here—cheese for me me me me." Mr. Natalie had to round them all up and usher them out of the house.

This left just me, crouching on the kitchen floor, and Dusty, glowering at me from beneath the chair. I extended my hand a little farther toward him. My left hand—so in case I lost any fingers I could still hold a dinner fork.

But Dusty showed no interest in the morsel, no matter how much I dangled it or flapped it at him or pronounced upon its nummy-numminess. I decided to change tactics: I shut my mouth, sat stock-still, and left my arm suspended in place—like a statue of Mao, pointing boldly into a future of universal comradeship and olive-drab pajamas. The muscles in my shoulder were just beginning to twinge a bit when, finally, he put forward one tentative paw. Then another. Keeping a wary eye on me lest I spring suddenly to life, he crept toward me, his belly nearly grazing the floor, till he was within reach of the cheese. He then snatched it from my hand like a Venus flytrap and scurried back beneath the chair.

Emboldened by success, I waited till he was licking his chops, and then held out the next piece.

By these painstaking measures, I was able, over the course of several minutes, to not quite make friends with him, but establish a mutually beneficial relationship. I had cheese I clearly wished to dispose of; he was conditionally willing to take it off my hands. Not an inauspicious beginning. I know of marriages based on less.

It was getting late in the afternoon, and I still had a two-and-a-half-hour drive back to the city. Time to make a decision. I looked out the window at the other Shelties, who frolicked in the backyard as though convinced someone, somewhere, had a camcorder trained on them. They all seemed clever and ambitious and invincibly well adjusted. I could, I realized, take one of them instead.

I simply couldn't go through with it. The idea of once again bringing Dusty to the brink of adoption, only to toss him back at the final moment, was repellent to me. I didn't know exactly what happened to rescue dogs that proved unadoptable, but I could hazard an unpleasant guess. And I really didn't want that on my conscience.

I could always play for time—tell Natalie I needed a few more days to think about it. But I knew, even as I considered this, that I would not be making the drive to Bloomington again (unless perhaps I were fleeing the authorities, in which case this seemed like a pretty good place to go to ground). No, I really, honestly had to decide whether I'd be signing that contract or not, and I had to do it right now. I shut my eyes, took a deep breath, and listened as expectantly as Natalie to what was about to pass my lips.

On the long drive back home, Dusty sat beside me in the front of the car. Not the safest place for him, but whenever I placed him in back he leaped over into the passenger seat, so I decided not to bother fighting it. He sat bolt upright, his posture vastly more regal than the Wile E. Coyote skulking he'd done back at the foster house. He looked, well, handsome. Almost. Particularly if you gave him only a quick glance every now and then. And if you weren't wearing your glasses. And squinted.

He also drooled copiously and incessantly for the entire two hours and eleven minutes it took to reach the city—so much so that I feared he might drop dead from dehydration before I managed to get him home.

But he did not die. In fact his life was just gearing up.

CHAPTER 2

What the Dickens

When Jeffrey got home from work, he took one look at Dusty and said, "*That's* the new dog?" When I nodded, he took another, longer look and said, "What happened to it?"

"Nothing. What do you mean?"

"Just . . . Is it always going to look that way?"

So it wasn't quite love at first sight. Dusty didn't help matters by trying to dry hump Jeffrey's Coach briefcase or snarling at him when he tried to take it back. "You are *so* on your own," he said as he retreated to the relative safety of the TV room.

The days that followed brought only marginal improvement. Dusty was wary of his new surroundings and took his time accommodating himself to them, with one exception: he immediately marked all four corners of the backyard and thereafter fiercely defended them as though anyone who approached, human or canine, represented the most vicious threat imaginable. He exempted Carmen, as she was already firmly ensconced when he got there;

in fact he all but ignored her as he claimed the territory around her. All the while she watched him with a kind of quizzical tolerance, much as I imagine the Queen of England must have regarded Gandhi during his state visit to Buckingham Palace—and with, I'm sure, a similar question in her mind as to when this peculiar little string bean might be going on his way. In Dusty's case, of course, the answer was, "Never."

As the days passed, he rapidly extended the boundaries of his turf to include the street on which we lived; then the entire block; then the neighborhood *in toto*; and finally, heroically, to anywhere in the city I walked him. We would descend on some new frontier, he'd urinate posthaste on the nearest hedge, and that would be that: ownership had been transferred, sovereignty reassigned. Regime change by bladder release. And oh, by the way: terror alert is at orange.

He was, in fact, so viciously antisocial, so feral on our walks—I had to restrain him from attacking anyone who came within a dozen yards of us—that I e-mailed Natalie to inquire what, if anything, she knew of his history, which, in my blithe egoism, I'd neglected to ask about earlier. She sent back the bare facts of his prior life as she knew them. He apparently had spent most of his first year chained up outside a trailer adjacent to some train tracks in downstate Illinois, in which unvarying circumstances he survived driving rain, withering heat, and crippling cold until someone—presumably the neighbors who must exist even at this degree of isolation—either reported this case of naked neglect or simply took him from the premises without asking permission; Natalie wasn't sure which. Either way, he ended up in the custody of the rescue society.

For some time after learning this, I couldn't look at him without lapsing into pity over what I imagined was a puppyhood of Dickensian privation. That he hadn't come through it with the undimmed good nature of an Oliver Twist or Nicholas Nickelby, I couldn't really hold against him; after all it's hard enough to maintain faith in human nature when you're actually human. If you're an abused dog, forget about it.

And I believed he *was* abused. He had a special loathing of children; I quickly learned to shorten his leash whenever any of the neighborhood kids came barreling by. They would unfailingly ask, "Is he friendly?" and I would snap, "No!" a moment before Dusty himself snapped considerably more persuasively. When I first heard the circumstances of his early life, I had an aha moment, because, as I recall from my own childhood, there is nothing more irresistible to the prepubescent mob, no greater prod to its natural savagery, than a tethered animal. I was convinced that Dusty, when not enduring the brutal assault of the quixotic weather, had had to contend with the equally brutal assaults of underage gangs—their sticks, their stones, their slingshots and pellet guns.

I suddenly realized that I was indeed writing Dusty's story, but not the part that had inspired me to adopt him in the first place. It was time to work on that happy ending—and that meant fulfilling my role as his rescuer, in every sense. I was clearly his only hope. He had for so long guarded his little patch of ground and defended his life and limb against hostile forces that it was all he knew how to do; and now I'd brought him into an environment where he could magnify the scope of that task exponentially. He'd taken far too much responsibility on his bony little shoulders. I had to get him to cede that responsibility to me—to take *my* cues, look to *me* for direction—so that he could relax, could finally, and at long last, just be a dog.

So I signed him up for the first available obedience class. This had the added benefit of paving the way to agility training. Obedience develops the basic behaviors—sit, stay, heel, down, and the like—which help establish the authority over your dog that you'll need when you enter the agility ring.

But I worried about bringing him into in a room filled with other people and their dogs. Given the ferocity with which he confronted any newcomers on his daily rounds, how would he react to such a quantity of them all at once? Would he become so overwrought, so deranged, that I wouldn't be able to turn his attention back to me?

As it turned out, his viciousness was in direct proportion to the vulnerability of the threat at hand. A single jogger, a woman walking her beagle, a UPS deliveryman—these kinds of stray wanderers into his field of vision sent him into a tailspin of lethal rage. But when faced with a dozen strangers, each accompanied by a canine of often impressive size, something in him short-circuited. He shut down almost to the point of catatonia. In fact I was a little embarrassed that first night of class; on my application form, under the question "What would you like to accomplish with your dog in this course?" I'd written, "To curb his aggression and put a brake on his hair-trigger temper." When the instructor, a woman named Jan who dressed like a high school basketball coach, had each of us make an introduction to the rest of the group, she stopped after my turn and said, "This is Dusty? This is the savage man-eater you want me to tame?" In response, Dusty peered out at her from where he cowered behind my calves.

It was a paradox, certainly, but I wasn't about to question it, since it made him more tractable in class. So far from fulfilling my fear that he might lunge at anyone who came near to us, he pressed himself against my legs and darted terrified glances at the yapping multitude around him.

While this certainly helped me control him in class—he willingly stuck by me and remained more or less attuned to whatever I said to him (though he was often distracted by the barking and brawling of other less-inhibited dogs)—it didn't solve my original problem, which was his own highly selective aggression. It never failed that, after an hour of teaching him to sit, stay, and heel, all of which he mastered quickly and meekly, no sooner did he get all four paws into his own backyard than he would devolve once more into the beast of the Apocalypse, baying for the blood of innocent passersby.

I expressed my frustration to Jan, who listened patiently if a tad dubiously. "Give it time," she said. "He may not be exhibiting aggression in class, but he is learning to defer to you. You're gradually becoming his alpha figure. There's an alpha male in every dog pack who rules the roost. The more you work on obedience exercises at home, the more quickly he'll learn to translate your authority to that area of his life, and then you'll have the tools to deal with his aggression on your own."

So we practiced at home. I put him through the same paces we went through in class each week. I hooked him up to a ten-foot leash, and leaving it slack I allowed him the freedom of the yard. Then I called, "Dusty, come!" And when he ignored me, I started reining in the leash, physically pulling him to me—all the while reinforcing his approach by saying, "Good boy, good boy, good boy!" (which presumably he could hear over his guttural choking) and then giving him a treat when he finally reached me. And what do you know, it worked as well as it did in class: he eventually got the message that when I called him resistance would be both futile and unpleasant, whereas compliance would be pleasant and profitable. In no time at all, he was coming to me of his own volition; I no longer had to reel him in like a nineteen-pound mackerel.

That is, except when some vicious threat appeared across the fence. Say, the mailman or a pizza-delivery boy or someone who had the sheer galling nerve to actually live next door. In that case Dusty exploded into cacophonous fury, unable or unwilling to hear me shout, "Come, come!" and resisting mightily when I hauled him in, to the point of actually strangling himself. More than once his tongue turned black, and on one memorable occasion he actually blacked out—keeled over as if someone had shot him. (Fortunately, I'm not faint of heart about such things, having passed out a fair amount myself during my college days.)

And all the while, Carmen lay several yards away, watching with sphinxlike serenity and a look in her eye that was almost mocking. "This is my replacement?" she seemed to say. "This is the future champion? Mm-hmm. Good luck with that."

CHAPTER 3

Class Struggle

I told Dee I'd be returning to her agility class with a new Sheltie, and when I walked in on the first night, she did a kind of double take. I suppose she was expecting another Carmen, whom she'd nicknamed the Diva for her habit of pausing in midperformance to glance approvingly at her reflection. Clearly, my new dog had no reason to be quite so fond of mirrors.

"Well, hey there, Dusty," she said after I'd introduced him. "You've got a lot to live up to; your big sister is pretty special." She leaned down to pet him, and he backed away like she'd come at him with a blowtorch.

This pretty much established the tone of their relationship for the next year and a half.

Dee held three agility classes every Thursday night: a beginners' session at seven, an intermediate at eight, and an advanced at nine. I'd worked my way up to advanced with Carmen, but now I was back in beginners, along with several other newbies and a few especially dense or difficult dogs who were returning for another go-round at the basics. (If I let myself sneer in derision at them, rest assured my karmic payback was not long in coming.)

The equipment was all set up and I was eager to test Dusty's mettle against the teeter or the chute, but this first class was almost entirely devoted to establishing some guiding principles. Dee didn't get into much of the background and history of agility—I suppose that might've been too much for a room filled with squirming dogs on taut leashes—but, thanks to my spate of Internet research before signing up Carmen, I already had a pretty good grasp on that.

The sport's origins date back to 1978, when a British dog-show producer named John Varley was charged with finding something to fill the dead time between the end of obedience championships and the start of "group breed" judging. Drawing on his prior experience in equestrian trials, he came up with a series of intricate obstacle courses through which dogs ran, jumped, and climbed to the finish line. It was fast, fun, and the crowd went nuts for it. The next year it was added to the program as its own dedicated event, and thereafter went wide-screen all across the United Kingdom. In 1986 Kenneth Tatsch, a Texas dog lover, seeing it for the first time and sensing its potential in this country, hurried home and founded the first American agility club, the United States Dog Agility Association. Soon there were more than a dozen others, hosting trials all year round, all across the country. The American Kennel Club (AKC), not about to be left out, embraced agility and is now the predominate presence in the sport. AKC trials are open to only purebred dogs, but there are other organizations, such as the North American Dog Agility Council (NADAC) and Canine Performance Events, that allow competition by mixed breeds and by breeds that aren't recognized by the snooty old AKC.

In short order canine agility became one of the fastest-growing sports in America. Now it's even attracted its first celebrity contestant, the Olympic gold medalist Greg Louganis—who has not, as of this writing, gone quite as far in agility as he did in diving. (Nor has he cracked his head against the A-frame, so let's call it a draw.)

It turns out that I myself was the celebrity in Dee's new beginners' class. She'd occasionally punctuate her pointers on how to approach the obstacles by saying, "Just ask Rob—he's already trained another dog and even competed with her," and the students would crane their necks and look at me reappraisingly.

But any authority I might initially have had melted away over the following weeks. Carmen had been a quick study, grasping what was required of her and improving it on each successive go-round. Dusty, on the other hand, in his general trepidation over being in the same room with so many potential arch-nemeses, seemed to forget everything I told him the moment I stopped talking.

The training started with the easiest of the obstacles: jumping. All dogs jump, so in theory it's simply a matter of teaching them to do it on command. There are several kinds of jump used in agility trials, including the standard bar jumps, double jumps (two bar jumps abutting one another), wing jumps (with extensions on either side of the bars), panel jumps (with wooden slats in place of a bar), and so on. What they have in common is that they can be raised or lowered from eight to twenty-six inches, to accommodate different-sized dogs. Competitions are divided by bar height: dogs that jump at twenty-four inches are pitted against other twenty-fours, and so on.

Since Dusty was roughly the same size as Carmen, I knew he'd be jumping at sixteen inches. There were a few other sixteen-inch dogs in class, as well as twenties, twenty-fours, and a couple of twelves. No eights (which was a relief; some of the larger dogs on hand looked like they'd happily eat an eight). But here, at the outset, we set the bar at twelve for all the dogs so that their natural inclination, when they came up to it, would be to hop over it. As Dusty and I approached, I said, "Over!" so that he would begin to associate this command with the move he was about to make. Except he didn't make it. He stopped short, glanced at the bar, then glared up at me—as I tugged gently at his leash from a few paces beyond—shooting me a look that said, "How do you expect me to follow you when there's this large metal impediment in the way?"

I must have appeared flummoxed, and I was: Carmen hadn't had this trouble—she'd cleared her first bar as though she'd been waiting her whole life to do it. "It's okay," Dee said. One of her shining qualities is that she's rarely discouraged (or at least she rarely shows it). "Try again, and this time you go over with him."

I blinked. "You . . . you want *me* to jump over the bar?"

"Yup. Show him how to do it."

I hesitated a moment; but only a moment. If I was out to produce a champion, I couldn't fold at the first hitch in the training. There would be greater sacrifices required of me, I was sure, than a simple loss of dignity.

I took Dusty by the leash, walked him back to the approach, and then together we trotted up to the jump. "Over!" I cried, and I hurled all 180-odd pounds of my bulk up and across the bar. I could feel my feet dangle in the air. I must have looked like a massive, spastic marionette. Then I landed with an *oof,* turned my head, and saw Dusty seated primly on the far side of the jump, his head slightly turned away from me as though to reassure any on-looker, "Hey, I barely know the guy."

Eventually—long after all the other dogs in the class were leaping to and fro over their bars, and the class looked like the Martha Graham Dance Company celebrating the joys of spring—Dusty finally got it. The metaphoric lightbulb over his head switched on, and he sailed easily over the jump. I praised him profusely, the high pitch of my voice betraying my obvious relief and also costing me a little more of my dwindling reserves of manhood. We did the jump again, and then again. Then we raised the bar to sixteen inches, where Dusy would be competing—if we ever got to competition, which wasn't something I'd have bet cash money on right at the moment. He nailed it. Then he nailed it again.

"Okay," said Dee, clearly happy to be making progress at last after so much effort, "try it without the leash."

I unhooked him and commanded him to sit and stay; then I went to the other side of the jump, looked him dead in the eye, conveying all the authority I could muster, and said, "Dusty, over!"

He turned the opposite direction and made a mad dash across the room, vaulting over the gate and into the lobby.

I looked at Dee sheepishly. "Well," I said, "he did jump."

CHAPTER 4

Dee-lightful

Of course Dusty and I weren't the most difficult team Dee had ever trained. There were plenty of dogs whose exuberance could not easily be funneled into a structured activity, and there were handlers whose thickness made your average two-by-four look like Stephen Hawking. "Try that again with the dog on your right," Dee would call out after a botched jump, which the handler would then repeat in exactly the same way. "Your other right," Dee inevitably corrected him. Her patience seemed, well, not infinite; occasionally she'd get steamed, but never by forgetfulness or clumsiness or even stupidity. The only times she'd come close to losing her religion were when people casually abandoned their dogs on the course. When one such handler snarked about how her Shiba Inu should "know better" than to screw up, Dee would have none of it. "He *doesn't* know better," she snapped, the set of her jaw forbidding all argument. "That's why you're out there. That's your job. To *help* him."

She never let us forget that this was an activity for dogs, which meant that their enjoyment was paramount. She wouldn't allow any scolding, rebuking, or, God forbid, striking of the animals. Whatever they learned would be learned through encouragement and praise. They would have *fun*.

She had the imperturbability of a medieval saint, spiced with the whiplash wit of a 1940s movie sidekick. She was a North Side Chicago girl, born and bred, which explained both her grit and her grin; it's a tough breed but a good-humored one. She had a typical midwestern face too—open, earnest, bright—and I never knew her to muddy its sunniness with makeup. It helped enormously, when your dog was subverting your every attempt to enlighten him on some point or other, to have such a face over your shoulder, cheering you on. Even more encouraging was her back-length blond ponytail—by far her defining feature—which would wag like a tail when she wildly applauded your hard-earned successes.

Like most dog people, Dee had a special affinity for a certain breed, and as is often the case, the affinity was cemented in childhood. Ironically, the fateful introduction almost didn't happen. When she was seven, her family set out to adopt a collie but had to renege because of her mother's allergies. (As a collie lover, I have to wonder why they didn't just replace the mother.) A miniature poodle was then considered but rejected as too small. Finally, they found a breed both the right size and suitably hypoallergenic: the Airedale, king of terriers. A female named Annie came into Dee's life and set in motion an enduring love affair.

Airedales—and dogs in general—were a constant in her life ever after. Her college boyfriend (now her husband) gave her a puppy for graduation, and so her subsequent identity-seeking years—which find most of us drifting temporarily away from the profound canine friendships of our childhood (and into the kind of behaviors we have to spend the next few decades living down, if not surgically correcting)—benefited from the constant presence of at least one indestructible touchstone.

And Dee did indeed undertake some extensive identity seeking, passing through both law school and a spell as a dancer. She wouldn't readily admit to the former ("I don't want people to judge me," she quipped) but credited the latter with giving her a head start on building her agility prowess. In fact she claimed to be able to tell which of her students had also trained in dance—or gymnastics or the martial arts or any similar endeavor. They possessed a kind of integrated, whole-body awareness that made them agility naturals. I longed for Dee to ask, after marveling at one of my runs, whether I'd studied karate or participated in any triathlons, but the most she ever asked me were things like "Do you want to sit down and catch your breath?"

Marriage to a breadwinning husband provided her the luxury of time to discover her destined place in the world. But even as she wafted through a succession of office jobs, the future was never really in doubt—just waiting for her to stumble on to it. In fact, almost literally so. Among the handful of possessions to survive her transition from childhood to adulthood was a copy of the pioneering text *The Koehler Method of Dog Training*—a method she later came to regard as too "yank 'em and crank 'em" but whose presence among her belongings was a testament to her early interest in the pursuit that would become her career.

Even as Dee's professional life remained in stasis, her immersion in the dog world deepened. With her new Airedale, Mariah, she competed in both obedience and conformation (the Westminster-style best-of-breed trials). This was, she hastened to point out, "Before I knew better," as Mariah was too short ever to embody the breed standard. (She'd have better luck with her next Airedale, Darby.) But she was so successful at obedience that she ended up teaching classes for the Chicago Park District—her first foray into the world of professional coaching.

When agility reached the Midwest, Dee got into that as well, though in those early days that meant driving way the hell out to places like Antioch or Naperville—places where you thought twice about pulling in for gas because what if they don't like your kind in these here parts—and that was just to train, never mind compete. Undaunted, she mastered the basics and entered trials sponsored by various clubs, including NADAC and UKC and other alphabet pileups, and became familiar with the full breadth of the sport's terrain. She found herself most comfortable in the AKC and focused her energies there. Before long Dee found herself in the upper echelons of the sport.

When the Windy City K-9 Club opened on Chicago's North Side in the mid-1980s, she had an impressive enough résumé to work a deal whereby she conducted agility classes on its premises twice a week. Some of her first students—Marilyn, Andi, Bruce—remained faithful disciples and provided the foundation for what Dee decided to call All Fours Dog Training. The group even developed its own logo and a Web site with the rather characterless address of chicagoagility.com. (As Dee tells it, she and her husband, Keith, had typed "allfours.com" into their browser to see if the URL was available. "Lo and behold, up comes a porn site! I had to warn all my students not to go there. But every once in a while I'll catch Keith looking at it and he'll be all, 'Oh, I was just checking to see if the address is still taken.'")

It was a testament to Dee's sense of humor and ability to inspire devotion that on my return to agility I encountered so many people I'd known before. Some, like me, were training brand-new dogs. (This included Dee herself, who was now partnered with Darby's heir, an irrepressible female named Kaleigh.) It was also revealing to note that Dee's methods had evolved. This was not a woman ever likely to become set in her ways or to ignore new ideas and advances in other quarters.

For instance, back when I trained Carmen, Dee had a certain way of teaching the weave poles—a row of twelve upright masts the dog must negotiate slalom-style. To achieve this, Dee set the poles in two rows of six and then had the handler call the dog through the space between them. With each pass, the rows would be moved closer together, till eventually the dog couldn't maneuver between them anymore and had to snake through them like a cat around someone's ankles. It worked well enough; Carmen became a very proficient weaver. At her peak she even banked, like a skier.

Dee's new weave-pole method was radically different. It started with just two poles, and the idea was to get the dog to pass through them correctly; i.e., leading with the left shoulder. The theory being that once the dog has the principle down the succeeding poles will just fall into line. At the heart of this approach is the notion that the dog has to figure out the poles for herself—even in the absence of a verbal command. That means breaking down the weave-pole entry into very small components and rewarding each one. For example, you reward the dog if she looks at the weave poles. Once she figures out that turning her head that way earns a treat, you stop. Now she has to figure out what *additional* behavior you want to add to the first. She might run through a variety of possible solutions, but the moment she turns and steps toward the weave poles, you give her a new treat. Eventually, incrementally, the dog gets the idea that going through those poles is a damn fine thing to do, and could she have another Snausage please?

This makes for a long, tedious process, and occasionally a largish wallop of existential despair, but in the end you get your dog to make a perfect weave-pole entry time after time and, most importantly, it was *her* idea. She figured it out herself, you never once commanded her. This is something of a quantum leap, training-wise, and informed much of what Dee now passed along to us. What it did was take the dogs from a place where they were obeying orders to one where they were thinking independently—acting instead of reacting.

Dusty took longer than the other dogs to reach this milestone because he disdained all material inducements. You might have called him monastic had his anxiety level not been ratchetted so high; you only find monks this nervous in Boccaccio. He sat by the two weave poles and looked, not at me, but at everyone else around him in a dither of distress. My job was to reward him the moment he made the slightest gesture toward the entry pole, but his eyes were darting too fast for me to follow, and besides I had no means of rewarding him beyond praise, and he wasn't listening to me. We stood there, twitching and flailing as Dee made the rounds, checking on everybody's progress, so that I was in a something of a lather myself by the time she reached us.

"How's Dusty doin'?" she asked—just as Dusty nearly toppled over from leaning away at her approach.

"We seem to be having trouble," I said.

"What kind of trouble?"

"Well, basically, existing on the same planet."

She gave me a come-on-now smirk and rolled up her sleeves. Then she took us through the whole process in baby steps, and by the end of the hour had Dusty making a solid weave-pole entry two times out of three.

"He's a good boy," Dee said. "Bless his heart."

A Southern friend once told me that "bless his heart" is Dixie code for "he's so stupid." Since Dee is a Chicago gal, I figured she might mean something different. Anyway, I was too grateful to argue. Somehow the scattered pieces of our enterprise had been gathered together and we had been forged into a team—exhausted and gasping and streaming with sweat, sure, but still a team.

And Dee, it was now blindingly apparent to me, was a woman who had found her true calling.

CHAPTER 5

The Obstacles of My Affections

Dusty and I spent a year and a half slowly building proficiency, speed, and (theoretically) mastery of the ten obstacles that comprise an agility course. I've alluded to these before, but, to convey exactly what mastering them involves, I'll describe them a tad more explicitly. In no particular order, we have:

The A-frame: Two large platforms, about three feet wide, hinged together to form an A (hence the name). The dog's job is to climb up one side, then descend the other. Sounds easy, but this baby gets *steep*—between five and six feet. Sometimes bigger dogs, when their center of gravity tilts too far, can find themselves skittering down on their stomachs, like it's a waterslide.

The dog walk: Three planks, eight to twelve feet long and about a foot wide, joined so that the center plank is roughly four feet off the ground. As with the A-frame, the dog must traverse its length.

Jumps: Just to recap, several kinds are used in trials, of different materials and widths. Each bar can be raised or lowered, from eight to twenty-four inches, depending on the dog's height at the withers. Knocking a bar off its frame is an immediate NQ. It's also very embarrassing for the handler—sort of like farting in church.

Broad jumps: Same principle as the above, only the emphasis is on the length of the jump rather than its height. The dog jumps horizontally over a row of slats, rather than vertically over a bar.

The tire: A big rubber tire is suspended in a frame, and in order to qualify a dog has to leap through it—sort of like Siegfried and Roy's tigers hurtling through a hoop, albeit without the fire. As with the jumps, the tire can be raised or lowered, from eight to twenty-four inches, to accommodate different sized dogs.

The teeter (also known as a seesaw): Pretty similar to the device you rode on as a kid, only without seats. It's anywhere between ten and twelve feet long. The dog is required to ascend the weighted end, then descend once she's past the midpoint and her own weight causes the other side to lower. Often when a very small dog tackles this obstacle, her weight proves insufficient to lower the far end until she's were well past the axis; this results in *quite* an unnerving slam. Dusty liked the teeter least, for this very reason. I think the first time he did it, it scared him out of a year's growth, which, being a Sheltie, he could ill afford.

The tunnel: A large tube, ten to twenty feet long and about two feet in diameter, made of vinyl stretched over a wire ribbing so that it can be bent into a U and shortened or lengthened as desired. Dogs must simply go in one end and come out the other. But when the tunnel is curved, and the end isn't visible from the entry, many dogs instinctively balk. Sometimes a shy dog will choose to go in and not come out again, in which case her handler often has to crawl in after her. For this reason, I strongly advise against the wearing of short shorts.

The chute (also called the "collapsed tunnel"): A large cylinder, with a two-foot-wide opening, connected to an expanse of canvas or cloth about twelve feet long. The dog has to barrel through this, essentially blind since the canvas is clinging to her. Sometimes a dog panics, tries to back up, and gets tangled in the fabric and starts to thrash. This can be a little upsetting to more sensitive souls. Try not to whimper; the larger dogs might sense your weakness and devour you (larger handlers too).

The table: Sometimes called the "pause table," because it's where you direct your dog to stop and sit (or to assume a down position—the judge decides which at the beginning of a run). It can be tough to get a dog to break her momentum and remain still for what feels like a small eternity while the judge counts down from five. The table is about three feet square, and the height is adjustable. For some reason, certain dogs like to take a dump on this obstacle. I guess they figure, as long as they're up there doing nothing . . .

The weave poles: As described in the last chapter, these consist of a row of upright poles, about three feet high and spaced twenty inches apart, through which the dog maneuvers, slalom fashion. In competition the number of poles varies from six to twelve. The dog must always enter the poles with her left shoulder and exit with her right. This is one of the most difficult obstacles to teach a dog, because all the others involves skills she already possesses: all dogs jump, climb, burrow, and so on, but weaving between objects is an entirely new concept to the canine mind. In fact it's so difficult that a dog who successfully learns to weave on her handler's right may have to be retrained from scratch to do it on her left—which can make a grown handler break down and cry. Not that that's what I did. I'm just sayin'.

The good thing about these obstacles is that once you've got them down, you're set. They're the building blocks of every course you will ever run, from this point forward till the crack of doom (unless you compete outside the AKC, where you might find yourself faced with a swing plank or a crawl tunnel or, hell, for all I know platform diving and a javelin toss). Once you've mastered these ten obstacles, you'll spend the rest of your agility career working on the spaces *between* them—figuring out how best to guide your dog from one to the other with increasing speed and precision. You'll work endlessly on refining your gestures and commands and on honing the rapport with your dog that eventually turns you from two flailing bodies into a single cohesive unit: fast, fluid, and completely in synch. Ideally, anyway. We all still have our moments when we flop around like a fish on a pier.

The bad thing about the obstacles is that it's not all that easy to master them. There are any number of factors working against you, including your dog's size (when facing the narrow plank of the dog walk, a larger dog tends to resemble a bear on a tightrope), weight (heavier dogs have a harder time getting up the momentum to ascend the A-frame), and speed (more gung-ho dogs, like border collies, tend to overshoot the table or leap off the teeter or A-frame before having fully completed it). There are also setbacks due to accidents (getting tangled in the chute or falling off one of the taller obstacles can make a dog reluctant ever to go near them again), and of course there's always the issue of the dog's character (she might, for instance, be easily distracted or excessively timid or too fixated on the other dogs in the room).

But with patience and diligence—and a coach of genius, like Dee—you can overcome any difficulty and get your dog to the place you need her to be. One of the keys, of course, is knowing what her incentive is—what you can offer her in exchange for performing the way you want her to. For most dogs, it's food. With a treat in my hand, I could get Carmen to do anything. *Anything*. She'd go up and down an A-frame a dozen times in a row. She'd teeter till she tottered. She'd do back flips. She'd dial up a restaurant and book a table. In French.

Some dogs respond better to other stimuli. For example, many handlers bring a favorite pull toy to class with them, and at the end of a particular task reward their dogs with a brisk tugging session. Others throw a toy for the dog to retrieve. This seems to work best with retrievers, unsurprisingly. Some handlers find it sufficient simply to go in for a bit of playful roughhousing.

For Dusty, there was nothing. He responded to no incentive known to man. At home he liked food well enough, and was known to enjoy a bit of tugging. He'd even chase a ball now and then, with every appearance of emotional investment. And despite being only nineteen pounds, he liked it when I roughed him up a bit—flipped him on his back and ruffled his fur, and then tossed him aside like a bag of laundry. He'd scrabble up again and come charging back for more.

In class, however, his shutdown was so complete that none of these could rouse his notice, much less his interest. I tried cooking frankfurters and dicing them, then sticking them beneath his snout before working a particular obstacle. He'd give an obligatory sniff, as though obliged to by his DNA, then dismissively swivel his head away—leaving me with an oh-so-appealing handful of gristle and grease.

Likewise he turned up his nose at his favorite toys, the ones that, at home, he most liked to gnaw on and shake. And the one time I tried to praise him by grabbing him and slapping him around, he gave me a look of the sheerest horror, as though I were publicly ravishing him.

Dee was adamant. "You have to figure out what motivates him," she repeated time and again. "There must be *something*." But as weeks turned into months she dropped the subject, perhaps because—somehow, inexplicably—Dusty improved. It wasn't a miracle on the Our Lady of Fátima scale, but it felt damn close. He did what he was told. He jumped when I said "over," climbed the frame when I said "frame," came when I said "here," and plopped on the table when I said "down." He never once seemed to enjoy it—never got that look of wild delirium that comes over most dogs when they're performing at their peak—but I couldn't fault him otherwise. Maybe, I thought, if we just keep at it, the joy will come. Maybe he'll have an epiphany and his face will light up at the very sight of a wing jump. Or maybe I'm just a pageant mom.

In the meantime, he had most of the obstacles down solid (though the teeter remained touch and go). He stuck with me when we ran a course and kept a steady pace. There were worse dogs in the class, certainly—though most of them dropped out after a term or two. Dusty and I just kept going. Perhaps inevitably, Dee started applying some gentle pressure: "So when are you gonna run him? There's nothing like the experience of an actual competition to sharpen your skills." And equally inevitably, I found myself wavering. I'd wanted Dusty to be championship material *before* we began our quest to ascend the sport's highest pinnacle, but perhaps Dee was right—you don't achieve that kind of proficiency in the classroom, only in the ring.

And then one day, at the end of a lesson, she mentioned an upcoming trial in Crystal Lake. I'd been to that area many times with Jeffrey, who grew up just one township over, in rural Woodstock. Perhaps it was just this sliver of familiarity that made the prospect of competing suddenly more inviting.

I decided what the hell. We were ready.

And we were.

We *are*.

After a year and a half of training, we're *ready*.

Part Two

CHAPTER 6

A Measure of Difficulty

O n the road to our first trial. The drive is long and monoto-
nous. To fill the time I listen to orchestral music—the kind
of epic-length compositions that require sitting in place for a long
spell, a luxury modern life doesn't often afford. I haven't listened
to much serious music since college, when I thought that Schoen-
berg and Thelonious Monk were going to change the world.
Instead, thirty years later, all that's changed is me—a harried
middle-aged man trying to squeeze in some reconnection with the
infinite as I hurtle past cornfields on my way to chase glory with
my dog. And all in vain: as a child of the TV age, everything I hear
comes across as a soundtrack. While listening to Aaron Copland's
Billy the Kid suite, my mind drifts to the characters on *Deadwood*.

Eventually, we arrive at the Regional Sports Center, an indoor
facility that ordinarily hosts soccer and basketball games. It's a shame
the trial's not set up outdoors—it's a breezy, balmy September
day—but as I unload Dusty's crate and my canvas chair from the
trunk and tote them inside, I realize this may be a blessing. In a

show of team spirit, I've chosen to wear my All Fours Agility Team microfiber polo shirt, which was offered in only black. The fabric seems instantly to soak up all the available sun and magnify its warmth by a factor of ten. Sweat prickles up all over my body; within moments my face and back are streaming. If I were wearing this outside, I'd dehydrate in twenty minutes. The garment's much-touted wicking technology would essentially wick me away to a husk.

I run into Dee as soon as I enter; her ponytail swings briskly as she bustles across the facility. "Oh, good, you've got a tarp," she says, noticing the crinkly brown roll under my arm. "We can expand our turf."

"Turf" is our share of the crating area, which covers one of the complex's three courts. Tarps or mats are required so that the crates don't damage the floor, but they serve an additional, territorial purpose: by spreading them across the available space, we claim it for ourselves. This is important, because at indoor trials crating space is almost always at a premium. At peak hours it can be like Filene's Basement on bridal-sale day. And given that this is where the group will hang out during the competition, snacking and gabbing and comparing notes on our runs, we like to have a little leg room. What's more, it's Friday, meaning some people are at work today and won't be arriving till tomorrow. Got to save some space for them.

Dee leads me to the All Fours enclave, where a couple of colleagues are already encamped. But they're all running their dogs in the "excellent" class—the highest of three levels of competition—which makes them not so much colleagues as upperclassmen. They exist on a whole different experiential plane than I do.

I don't yet know who, if anyone, will be competing with me in the novice class.

I unfurl my tarp adjacent to the others, set up my crate and chair on its far corner, and then dash back to the car and collect Dusty, who's sitting in a pool of his own drool. He's clearly suffering some serious anxiety, but after a short walk in the parking lot (during which he contentedly sniffs the filthy pavement as I attempt not to think about the quasi-toxic crud that's ground into the concrete), he seems calmer—he's even smiling. But it's a ghastly smile, the kind you'd wear if someone you loathe showed up at your door uninvited.

When I think he's regained his equilibrium, I take him inside. Immediately, we're swarmed by dogs and handlers of all sizes— cigarette-thin men with gaunt-looking greyhounds, plus-sized gals trailing tiny papillons, metalheads with mastiffs, dykes with Dalmatians, huskies with huskies, and every other breed and body type imaginable, in every conceivable combination. A full third of the dogs are announcing their presence to the world in a cacophony of yelps, howls, snarls, and cries punctuated by sharp staccato barking. The density of the crowd is incredible, the clamor overwhelming, and I can only imagine the smell: a potent mixture of airborne hormones and tangy urine, thankfully beyond the feeble range of human detection but an overpowering wallop to canine nostrils.

I look down at Dusty. He seems about to swoon. Part of me would like to sweep him up in my arms and carry him above the fray, *protect* him. But that won't do. The boy is an athlete now. He's got to learn to man up. (Or dog up. Whatever.) I shorten the leash, command him to heel, and set out to take a look around the place.

The action has already begun on the courts set aside for competition. As in every AKC agility trial, there are two discrete rings: one, called "standard," is devoted to courses that incorporate all ten obstacles; the other, "jumpers with weaves" (just "jumpers" among the cognoscenti), sticks to, you guessed it, jumps and weaves (though a tunnel somehow always manages to sneak in).

Each course is designed by the judge who will preside over it; it is subsequently built by a staff of volunteers. There are usually a dozen to eighteen obstacles on any given course, and judges vary in how creatively they arrange them. They must also provide three variations of each course design, with differing degrees of difficulty, for the three separate classes, which are based on skill level: excellent, open, and novice. After each class runs, adjustments are made for the following group. Almost every trial begins with excellent, I suppose so that the elite competitors can leave when they're finished and enjoy the rest of the day. We novice handlers, by comparison, have to stick it out to the very end, when even the vendors have packed up and skedaddled.

Having scoped out the two rings, I pause to watch a few of the excellent teams run the jumpers course. Some, I'm glad to say, are as distracted and insubordinate as novices. I see dogs pull up short before taking an obstacle; this is called a "refusal." Others go for a different obstacle altogether, which is called an "off course." Both these faults detract from the total score. But most of the excellent dogs are really, well, excellent. They gracefully follow their handlers from the first obstacle to the last, and do it well under the time set by the judge. Their prowess is enviable. When you take first place in excellent, it *means* something.

I move on to the check-in table and get my armband. I also pick up some maps of the novice courses so I can study them while I'm waiting. It helps to go over them a few times on paper to determine in advance how best to approach your run: Start with the dog on your left or your right? Cross in front or behind, and where? That type of thing. Strategy.

From there we move on to our first big challenge: getting Dusty's official jump-height card—which will involve Dusty's height being measured, which will involve Dusty being touched by another human being.

There's no getting around it. If he doesn't go through this, any scores he earns today won't be recognized by the AKC. So I crouch down, give his ruff a good scratching, and say, "Be brave, okay? Big guy? *For me.*" And then I take him to the measuring table.

The woman in charge is one of those bespectacled, no-nonsense gals whose pink sweaters and henna highlights shouldn't fool you at all; they are military creatures down to the cellular level. I have to wait my turn as she crisply maneuvers her sliding scale to the withers of, first, a flat-coated retriever and then a keeshond, both of whom good-naturedly cooperate. There's an assembly-line efficiency to the proceedings, which is obviously the way she likes it. I begin to feel a slight sense of dread.

"Next," she says, as the keeshond spryly dismounts.

I hand her my form, then tell Dusty, "Up, boy," and give him a gentle tug. He backs away and tries to wriggle out of his collar. "No no," I say. "Come on, boy, up, *up.*"

He squirms even more frantically; he's working himself into a panic. In the meantime the table is empty, the clock is ticking, and there are three other people behind me with dogs waiting to be measured. "Hold on," I tell the woman with a forced smile, but in the split second I'm facing her Dusty gives one last contortion and frees himself from the collar. For a moment he's dazed by his success and just sits there blinking.

The woman waves the dog behind me onto the table while muttering something I don't quite catch and probably don't want repeated. I grab Dusty just as he begins to slink away, reattach his collar, and get back at the head of the line. When the table opens up again, I take no chances, physically carrying him over and placing him atop it. "It's okay, boy," I tell him as his pupils dilate. "It's fine. Everything's fine."

"He needs to be standing upright," says the woman with all the bedside manner of George S. Patton. I get the feeling if we don't cooperate she'll slap me. Dusty's back legs are splayed. I straighten them with my hands, then take his torso and align him with the scale, but when the woman extends an arm toward him, he leans into me so that he's standing at a sixty-degree angle.

"*Upright*, please," she says, and I try to comply, I really do, but Dusty is essentially limp. I push him away from me and his knees buckle. I hold him up by the trunk and his legs collapse altogether, like a marionette's.

By this time there are impatient rustlings behind me, and I'm sweating so freely that my shirt can't wick fast enough. Dusty keeps leaning into me, his terror of both the measuring device and the measurer herself steadily mounting. I'm running out of ideas. In desperation, I figure that if he doesn't have me to lean against he won't be able to lean at all, so I move aside. He leans anyway and plummets right off the table, landing on the floor with a *whumpf*.

The woman waves up the next dog, and I surprise myself by

lashing out my arm and saying no in a way that causes her to look at me with a degree of wary respect from behind her purple-framed bifocals. I pick up Dusty, slap him back onto the table, and through clenched teeth command him to *stay*. My suddenly gestapo-like demeanor takes him by surprise just long enough for the woman to scroll the scale down to his shoulder and get a reading: 17.25 inches. Then he goes all rag-doll again, but it's okay; we've got what we needed.

The woman completes and signs my form. I thank her for her time, tuck Dusty under my arm like a parcel, and march away with whatever dignity I haven't already sweated down my back. I feel dehydrated and unmanned. It looks to be a long, long day.

After a few yards I grow tired of carrying him, so I pause to lower him back to the floor. A passerby does a double take, then stops and says, "Cryptic blue?"

I cock my head. "Excuse me?"

She points to Dusty. "Cryptic blue?"

For a giddy moment I feel like an undercover agent in some Soviet-era espionage film; like I'm meant to respond, "The cry of the lark diminishes at vespers," then hastily exchange manila files of classified documents. But instead I say, "Uh, no, his name's Dusty."

She smiles at my confusion. "He's a cryptic blue," she says. "His coloring," she explains, when I continue to appear bewildered.

"Oh," I say, finally catching on. "I thought he was a tricolor."

She shakes her head and tries to move in closer; Dusty responds by actually withdrawing into himself like a tortoise. I'm quite impressed. I didn't know his skeleton could work that way. She's not at all dismayed by the rebuff. "Cryptic blue," she repeats. "It's actually closer to blue merle than tri, but really it's neither. He's his own special blend."

I look anew at the ash-colored highlights of Dusty's coat. "No kidding. I thought he was just prematurely gray or something."

"Oh, no. Much prettier than gray." She smiles at Dusty. "Very rare, cryptic blues. Can't remember the last time I saw one. Where'd you get him?"

"Actually, he's a rescue." Her eyebrows arch; she seems surprised at the idea that someone actually gave up a cryptic blue. "It's our first trial," I add, not knowing what else to say.

"Well, good luck to you. And good luck to *you*, Dusty." Then with a wink she continues on her way.

"Hear that, boy?" I tell him as I lead him back to the crating area. "You're not just any run-of-the-mill Sheltie, here. You're a *cryptic blue*."

Coming so soon after the measuring-table fiasco, this seems to augur well for the day. But Dusty appears signally unimpressed.

Back at the All Fours turf, I pop him in his crate, lowering the flaps over the sides so he doesn't feel exposed and vulnerable in the midst of all these passing strangers; he is transparently relieved. I give him a bowl of water, and he falls into a little ash-colored heap, like I've just let all the air out of him.

There are more people here now, and I get my first look at my fellow novice handlers. These are the people against whom I will be judging myself, and accordingly I feel a little surge of competitive jealousy. "Today I mop the floor with you," I think as I greet them with a big, toothpaste-ad grin. I don't know why I need to feel this way—that these people are threats who must be abolished. They can't prevent me from getting a first-place score, because they're not jumping at my height. Whether I become king of the sixteens has nothing to do with how well or poorly they perform. And yet I feel driven to it. It's similar to what I feel whenever I jog around my neighborhood park and some guy comes running toward me from the opposite direction. At the exact spot where we intersect, I'll look across the park to the corresponding point on the opposite side—then quicken my pace to get there first, because if I do, it means *I'm faster*. I don't know the guy, of course—will probably never see him again—but it matters desperately that I prove myself better than him. Testosterone: it's a blessing; it's a curse.

There are three other novice competitors, and I must choose one of them to be my prod—my adversary. There's Sue, a tall, fresh-faced woman who's running her rottweiler, Norris. There's also Carl and Kim, a young husband-and-wife combo handling Portuguese water dogs, Fletcher and KC.

Strictly speaking, I ought to pit myself against Sue, since she, like me, has previously had another dog in competition, giving us both prior ring experience. But looking at her now, she just won't do. She's too pretty—too girly. It's not that I don't think she's a worthy competitor; you don't train and handle rottweilers without some iron in your spine. But this is basically about creative visualization, and when I conjure up an image of my opponent lying vanquished at my feet, I don't want to see someone in a halter top and headband. I want a brawny, barrel-chested, hairy-armed *hombre*. So it must be Carl.

And besides, Sue has run Norris at other trials. But this is Carl and Kim's first, just as it's mine with Dusty. So there's that to consider. We're both starting at the same time, from the same place.

I've observed Carl in class; I know he's got drive, a kind of fierceness that's exactly what I'm looking for to spur me on. Not to mention his cold, clear eyes, which are almost wolflike. His wife, Kim, by contrast, is more serene, the way so many women are. She's self-contained, imperturbable. Dark-haired, dark-eyed, her smooth face betraying no history of intense emotion—she seems majestically internalized. Her eyes are always focused on the middle distance, as if part of her isn't entirely here. Clearly she has nothing to prove. Carl, like a lot of men, acts as though he has everything to prove, and that his life depends on it. He fidgets. He paces. He nearly sizzles with competitive energy.

I peer in at Dusty, curled up like a croissant in the corner of his crate, and I send him a telepathic message: "Whatever we do out there, we must be better than Carl and Fletcher. You hear me, boy? The cryptic blue must rule! We must leave them gasping and broken in the miserable wreckage of their defeat."

Dusty heaves a little sigh. I decide to take this as agreement: Message received. Game on!

CHAPTER 7

The Agony and the Agony

As a general rule, when you have to tell yourself that something wasn't a complete disaster, probably what you've had is a complete disaster.

Which brings us to Dusty's first run. Jumpers with weaves—a course I honestly think he has a decent chance of acing. It's just jumps, right? With weaves. Okay, the weaves are problematic, but in novice you get to go back and retry them if you screw up, even half a dozen times if you think it'll do any good; plus, we've put in all that practice time weaving in the backyard. And the jumps—what's to worry? It's a bar. You jump over it.

At least that's the theory. But as I really ought to know by now, theory and practice can be as different as apples and oil tankers. Particularly where Dusty's concerned.

We begin well: I get him set up perfectly at the starting line, and he holds his sit-stay like a real champ. When I get the nod from the timekeeper to begin, I lead him out to the first jump and call, "Over!" He behaves as if both the concept and the word are completely alien to him. He circles the jump, looks right past the bar, at one point even ducks under it—and the more I shout "Over!" the more the command seems to turn to butterflies in the air and cavort about his head without ever touching him.

And thus it goes for pretty much the whole course. Dusty's first balk has a domino effect. I balk in anticipation of him balking at the second jump, so he of course balks too. And after that, well, we're basically balkanized. Halfway through he does execute a half-hearted jump, which not only knocks down the bar but both sides of its frame as well. I can feel the love from the course setters; it flows warmly over me, like napalm.

Prior to the judging, as is the custom, we were allowed to walk the course, and I did so a dozen times, plotting out how best to tackle it. There are fifteen obstacles altogether, basically arranged to form a figure eight. "Front cross after obstacle nine," I told myself. "Handle from the left starting at obstacle thirteen." The idea is always to keep yourself on the inside track so that you don't have to run as fast as your dog (since, probably, you can't anyway). By the time I finished walking the course, I had my attack down with mathematic precision.

And now, in the heat of the moment, it's dissolving like Alka-Seltzer. I'm having a lesson in how different training and competition can be. Everything changes when it's for real—when the judge is out there with you and the clock is running and they're watching you out in the stands. The whole nature of time seems radically to alter: sometimes it speeds up so that you don't know where you are or how you got there; sometimes it slows down so that you seriously think you'll be stuck in a four-second loop for the remainder of eternity.

By the time I get Dusty past the final jump and lurch, gasping, off the course, I'm a different man: older, feebler, more at risk of incontinence. But Dee is right there with a kind word. "Not a bad job!" she says, grinning with such sincerity that, I can't help it, I believe her. "Man, he really nailed those weave poles!" Which is of course the bitter irony. He whisked through those six poles like he could've done sixty more. It was just the jumps—which he could do in his goddamn sleep—that proved insurmountable.

But I feel immeasurably bucked up by Dee's words. And it occurs to me then: she's handling me like she teaches us to handle the dogs. Her mantra is always: "Make it fun. Find something to praise. Concentrate on what your dog does right, not on what she does wrong."

I feel a brief flurry of indignation, till I realize, what the hell, whatever works. And really, does a starving man turn down a nice, fresh handout? Not this starving man, and please pass the salt and pepper. On my way back to the crating area I run into Sue, who asks, "How'd you do?" I beam her a big smile and say, "We really nailed the weave poles!"

I return Dusty to his crate. He immediately curls up and shuts his eyes. Apparently I've worn him out. Suddenly, I realize what this morning has been like for him: I've dragged him to a place where there's not a single familiar scent, hauled him into a giant concrete bunker filled with hundreds of other howling dogs, kept him zipped up in isolation for hours, then yanked him onto an agility course where I confused him by being nervous and tentative and shouting commands at three times my normal volume. I couldn't have baffled him more if I'd started hurling bricks at him or burst into flame. And despite it all, he's done pretty well. I try to give him a biscuit, but he'll have none of it. He is disrespecting the hand that feeds him, and I can't say I blame him.

I'm the first of the All Fours novices to run this course, and the only sixteen-inch jumper. Now the bar goes up to twenty, and it's the bigger dogs' time to rumble. My fear, of course, is that my smoking ruin of a run has left the door wide open for Carl. "This must not be," I say, willing fate to bend to my will.

As I'm wishing him failure, Carl appears with Fletcher straining at the leash and sidles up beside me to make small talk. I blush for a moment, as though I've been busted. It can be very distracting to creative visualization, this unwillingness of others to play the parts you've assigned them in your head. Why isn't Carl psyching himself up to be as competitive with me as I am with him? I allow myself to consider that possibility from his point of view. Big mistake. After all, who am I to Carl? Some old bald guy from the last century, no doubt. He might ask me if I was at Studio 54—or, hell, Woodstock—but I doubt he'll ever see me as someone against whom he might test his mettle. "Ah, but he underestimates me at his cost," I think, supervillain style. I then make an effort to chat amicably, to keep him off his guard.

While Carl and I talk, his wife Kim has her first run with their other Portie, KC. It isn't a triumph. KC feels his freedom a little too keenly and goes on a tear around the ring, smiling at spectators and working the crowd like a politician. Eventually, Kim regains control of him and finishes the run respectably, but to do so she's had to shout out his name several times, which unfortunately catches Fletcher's attention. Hearing his mom's voice deranges him a little, and Carl has trouble even keeping hold of him.

And then Carl is on the line, and Fletcher—still twitchy and distracted—with him. Their run is every bit as chaotic as I could wish it. In fact maybe a bit more so. Instead of a figure eight, they end up sketching out several major constellations: Orion, Leo, both the Big and Little Dippers. Fate is serving up my order, all right, with a free side of onion rings. My inner supervillain can't resist a sinister *bwahahahaha!*

A few minutes later, when the bar goes up to twenty-four inches, Sue runs Norris to no better end. It's a clean sweep: the All Fours novices are off to a unanimously bad start.

Back at the crating space, there is much dissection and analysis of the various performances: where they went wrong and what steps might be taken to prevent similar failings in the next run. To my embarrassment, quite a bit more of this is devoted to the others than to me. For me there is just general praise: "Good first try!" "Not a bad job at all!" "Nothing to be ashamed of!" I feel like someone in a drawing class, whose teacher tells him, "Pretty colors! What a nice little horse and flowers!" before turning to the next student to dispense advice on shading and perspective.

I realize I'm being overly sensitive, probably as a result of having immersed myself in this minor endeavor with all the focus of Napoléon on his Russian campaign. I hook up Dusty and take him out for a pee break, then go to the car, roll down the windows, and sit there for thirty minutes with *The New York Times Book Review*, plowing through long, exhaustive reviews of novels I will almost certainly never read. Anything to pull me far away from the dismal performance Dusty's just put in.

By the time I return I've regained some perspective, and a good thing too because it's almost time for the standard course walkthrough. As ineptly as we handled jumpers, I expect no better from standard—in fact I actively fear worse, given the greater variety of obstacles. The teeter alone is enough to kill hope; Dusty has never loved this particular piece of equipment, and its fulcrum is set higher than he's yet encountered it in class. The slam it will make on the way down must register on the Richter scale.

Soon we're up, and despite my carefully planned moves Dusty chooses to chart an entirely different course. Perhaps he doesn't realize points aren't dispensed for originality. I shout at him. I plead. I cajole. And sometimes he deigns to acknowledge me, almost out of pity. But in general he treats me like a substitute teacher whose authority he can ignore with impunity. Again I leave the door wide open for Carl and Fletcher.

Fortunately, they fare no more happily. By now it's clear that having KC and Fletcher run back-to-back is a liability; while KC is on the course with Kim, Fletcher, hearing his mom's voice, works himself up into such a state that he's virtually unmanageable when his own turn comes up. Carl is frustrated and exhausted, and even Kim looks a bit strained.

And so the first day of competition ends with a nagging sense of failure and incipient despair.

Except for the dogs. They all seem just fine.

CHAPTER 8

Trial and Terror

Dinner is a subdued affair because I've returned home with only stories of defeat. But it's a nice night, the air is sweet and cool, and we can dine on the deck. Dusty usually isn't allowed out with us because he barks far too much, which prompts our neighbors on both sides to audibly and meaningfully shut their windows, but tonight he's flat on his flank, dead to the world. This is heartening to see; in my humble opinion, a tired dog is a good dog.

After dinner we adjourn to the TV room. Tonight's movie is Ridley Scott's *Gladiator*. I've chosen it because I'm a Roman-history buff, but its inaccuracies annoy me by being not only numerous but wildly implausible—just a few notches up from Bugs Bunny in *Roman Legion-Hare*. Still, its recreation of the actual city of Rome at its imperial zenith is dazzling, and the aerial shot of the Colosseum, brimming with spectators, knocks me for a loop. Unfortunately, I, like Dusty, am wiped out by the labors of the day, and by the time the major arena fights roll around I'm heavy lidded and fighting off sleep. During Russell Crowe's climactic battle with a man-eating tiger, my addled subconscious keeps looking for a teeter and A-frame in the background.

In the morning, I'm feeling renewed and refreshed, and buoyed by a strong urge for redemption. I itch to get back in the ring and take some serious charge. Dusty, however, is far less keen on the idea. He turns up his nose at breakfast, as though gambling on me not running him if his tank is on empty. But I grab a bag of salmon treats, leash him up, and take him out to the car. He sulks the whole way to the garage; he'd drag his heels, if he had any.

I tell myself, "He'll be more enthusiastic once he starts winning," but on reflection that doesn't really wash. After all, he gets praise from me no matter what kind of run he has, and after yesterday's comedy of errors I treated him like he'd qualified, taken first place, and found a cure for rickets. So how will he even know when he starts scoring? I suppose dogs are intelligent enough to pick up otherwise imperceptible cues, the kind that signify, for instance, that someone's genuinely happy instead of giving a Stanislavskian impression of happiness. Anyway, we'll find out soon enough. Possibly today!

The lot is full by the time I arrive, and I have to park across the road on the premises of a tree and garden center. It's Saturday, and quite a few more people are on hand to compete. In fact the cacophony makes yesterday's seem like the serene stillness of a NASCAR rally. Dusty is so intimidated that he seems to shrink with each step. If I don't get him to his crate fast, there may soon be nothing left of him.

The All Fours enclave is quite a bit more snug than I left it, due to several new arrivals. One of them is another novice competitor, Diane, who's here with her giant schnauzer, Annie. I don't see Carl or Kim, and for a moment I think I may need a new personal rival for the day. Despite the size of her dog, Diane just doesn't work for me. She's a lean, elegant lady with cascading salt-and-pepper hair, who makes everything she wears look like couture. This just doesn't square with the ideal adversary I've visualized—and who after last night looks a lot like Russell Crowe. Fortunately, Carl pops up from around the corner, bearing something from a vending machine, and I'm absolved from having to get all harsh on someone wearing Anne Klein.

Dee, as usual, is functioning as the master of the revels—she's slung low in her folding chair, gripping a big plastic cup of soda and entertaining those ranged around her with the story of how her husband, Keith, stepped in and ran Kaleigh for her when she had a broken ankle: "Oh, he did fine in standard, because—well, let's face it, all you have to do is say the name of an obstacle and Kaleigh'll go for it. So he came off the course all puffed up, like, 'This agility thing is no big deal'—just, y'know, a little condescending to me for going on and on about it all these years. And I was like, 'Right, fine,' but all the while I was thinking, 'Wait till you get to jumpers.' And of course he was a train wreck there. He'd say 'over' and his hand and his butt and his shoulders would be pointing to three separate jumps, so Kaleigh just decided which one she liked best, and after that she was off on a tear and Keith just stood there with his head spinning around, like, 'What, what? What?' He spent the entire run chasing her down. Anyway, we were supposed to go out to dinner afterward, but he barely made it back to the hotel. He collapsed on the bed and was zonked out for hours. With me sitting there in my cast, helpless and hungry. Nice."

Roars of laughter. Dee is a gifted storyteller, with a typically midwestern deadpan delivery seasoned by an occasional girlish squeak. And when she delivers a particularly juicy riposte, she jerks her head so that her ponytail swings in counterpoint. It's the perfect kicker and notches up the merriment every time.

But beyond her ability as a raconteuse, this story seems particularly geared to get a laugh from her present audience. Quite a few agility devotees are coupled, but usually to someone outside the sport; pairs like Carl and Kim are the exception rather than the rule. And there's an undercurrent of tension—slight but significant—when spouses are mentioned, the implication being, "Here I am again, spending a weekend with all of you instead of him/her, and what a shame he/she just *doesn't get it.*" In this way, I suppose agility people are no different from bowlers or boaters or garage-sale aficionados or others whose hobbies continually call them away from their families—sometimes hundreds of miles away. I know a woman whose fiancé runs a marathon every month, sometimes two. He has to travel all over the country and occasionally even abroad to manage it. And when he's not competing, he's training. She pretends to shrug it off good-naturedly, but you can tell it chafes, and of course as a listener you sympathize—his behavior sounds obsessive and crazy. But being in this kind of community—hearing Dee tweak her husband for "just not getting it" to gales of appreciative laughter—I can see the other side. No doubt Marathon Man and his buddies spend a lot of time joking about their significant others who just don't get it—who spend their free time, how, shopping? Going to movies? Lying on the couch watching *Dancing with the Stars?* Just letting the globe keep on spinning beneath them, ticking away the precious hours of their lives without ever once getting up, balling their fists, and hurling themselves at the biggest available challenge while screaming, "Cowabunga, baby!" Yeah, okay. I can see that side. I'm a little surprised that I do, given that only a year ago it was utterly alien to my nature; but now I completely understand the compelling urge to conquer.

Unfortunately, it isn't all about conquest. In fact when you factor in the down time at any given trial—hours and hours of it, dwarfing the six or seven minutes you'll actually find yourself in active competition—the daredevil aspect of the sport seems less prominent an attribute. But here's where another of its attractions comes into play: Fellowship. Camaraderie. The company of like minds. All those spouses who just don't get it—you can laugh about them here with impunity, because you are among your own kind. The hours spent in the crating area, slouched in your canvas chairs, ankles crossed, spines relaxed, chatting away about nothing while noshing endlessly on the cheapest food imaginable—this is all part of the sport's siren allure. What it amounts to is hanging out.

And this is where I face my own Everest. I've never been any good at hanging out. At least not in this kind of setting. Living on the North Side of Chicago, surrounding myself with friends who share my slightly rarefied perspective on life and how to live it, I forget just how far outside the mainstream I really am. But I can't forget it here. I'm a blue-state guy in a red-state world, and it seems every syllable I utter baldly reveals it. I try to pass as one of the gang, but I don't know how. Everywhere around me are people who follow *American Idol*; me, I've got a box at the Lyric Opera.

They read Tom Clancy; I read Tom Stoppard. They tack up posters of Brangelina; I've got a framed portrait of Barbe-Nicole Ponsardin, the "veuve" of Veuve Clicquot.

This was all fine when I was an agility tourist, showing up with Carmen like a visiting dignitary to run my two courses and then sail away. No doubt I was just another amusing blip on the fringes of the sport—the fancy man who actually used words like *albeit* and *notwithstanding* and who brought along vials of balsamic vinegar to dress his lunch. Not much different from the slender, pale youth whose body was covered with unambiguously violent tattoos or the woman whose enormous breasts, when she ran, made the exact slap-slap-slap of helicopter blades.

But I don't want to be a visiting freak anymore. I want to fit in. I want to be a member of the group in full and in earnest. Hell, I'm wearing the damn shirt! Which, I now notice, no one else is. Not that they need to; they all incontestably belong. Just listen to how their conversation weaves together, forming a seamless tapestry of anecdote and observation. I believe this is what's called "shooting the breeze." I can't do it. I can hold forth for twenty minutes on Italian neorealist films or the failures of FEMA, but I can't do this. I get restless. I shift; I squirm.

And, inevitably, I bolt. Which I prepare to do now, as their amiable banter whizzes over me like Molotov cocktails. When someone lobs a comment into my lap, I can only stare at it in terror. Sometimes I do manage to think of the right thing to say—but usually about two beats too late. Timing is everything in casual chatter, and the pace is both relentless and unforgiving. Quips fly; and so, now, do I.

I snap up copies of the novice courses I'll be running and take them outside to study; a happy plan, as it allows me both to use my time productively and to spend it out of doors (and away from the possibility of revealing—to myself if no one else—how ill suited I am to be part of anything that might remotely be called a "gang").

Like a woman holding up two possible outfits before a mirror, it's the kind of day that can't decide what season it wants to be; forehead-prickling sunshine is laced with cool autumnal breezes, while swirls of puffy seedlings are provided a soundtrack by the skittering of dead leaves across the concrete.

All very picturesque, certainly. But there's no place to sit down. There's the parking lot, and there's the big stucco building itself, bluntly and mercilessly demarcated like two incompatible states of being. Living in the city, where the streets and parks are filled with places to stop and pass the time, I always forget this quirk of the suburbs: the way the outdoors is treated merely as space between the indoors. You cross the exterior expanses only to get from one interior space to another. I can imagine the looks of bewilderment on the faces of my colleagues if they happened to find me out here. Why in God's name would I come all the way to the Crystal Lake Regional Sports Center and then *not go inside?* It's a basic dichotomy between urban and rural mind-sets. Trapped in crowded neighborhoods, living on top of one another, city folk can't wait for the weather to allow them to step outside of their confinement and breathe whatever fresh air filters down through the canyons of steel. Suburbanites, situated in enormous houses with rec rooms and home entertainment centers, and with the full weight of the natural world bearing down on them mercilessly from all sides, must dream of the day when they no longer have to go outside at all.

I suppose I could sit cross-legged on the tiny patch of lawn by the door; I'm still more than limber enough. But such a pose would be injurious to middle-aged dignity, unless you happen to be a middle-aged swami. I could also go sit in my car, but that would seem an admission of fear.

Still, it's fear I'm feeling. Why not say so? Social terror, is what it is. The inability to be at ease in a group of my chosen peers; the anxiety of not knowing what is expected of me.

It occurs to me that this is almost exactly one of Dusty's pathologies. Is it possible he caught it from me? Can he have picked up my nervousness, my urge to flee in such situations, and learned from it? I've made a vow to whip him into shape, to turn him into a champion, but he's only part of the team here. As his handler, I have to set the tone for our partnership.

I have to whip myself into shape too.

And that means facing up to my fear. It means turning back and rejoining my colleagues and sitting in my folding chair and risking maybe *not* getting some of their jokes and maybe saying something unwittingly pretentious and causing everyone to pause for a moment and exchange glances, and maybe accidentally saying something that offends one of them.

Then again, maybe I'd rather sit in the car after all.

No no, back I go. I've got a responsibility to Dusty, if not to myself.

Astonishingly, I find many of the group on their feet and headed away from the crating area—Carl, Kim, Diane, Sue. All the novices. "Jumpers walk-through," Diane tells me as she passes. I've been granted a reprieve!

I walk the course—another, more-lopsided figure eight, sixteen obstacles in *toto*—rehearsing my attack till I can close my eyes and run the course in my head.

And what do you know—Dusty's magic out there! He stays right with me, he heeds every command, he has only one refusal—it's like we're on fire.

I'm almost hyperventilating when I come off the course. Two of the excellent-class competitors, Betsy and Cyndi, are standing right by the exit gate; I can't understand why they don't look more excited.

"Did you see that?" I ask.

Cyndi happily nods. "He was really focused," she says. "It's great the way he's coming along!"

Coming along? What is she talking about? He was *perfect*. "Well, let me tell you," I say, giving Dusty a bear hug, "I'm really proud of him! This is his first Q!"

"Oh, he didn't Q," says Betsy.

I blink. Twice. "He didn't?"

"Oh, no," she says, as if explaining the law of gravity to someone flapping his arms and trying to fly. "He was over time."

"*Way* over," Cyndi chuckles with a roll of her eyes.

As it turns out, they aren't exaggerating. When the tallies are posted, I see to my horror that we were too long by almost twenty seconds. A small eternity. By the time we finished, some spectators must have needed a shave.

My only consolation is that Carl doesn't qualify with Fletcher either. But, like me with Dusty, he does disturbingly better than he did yesterday. A fact enthusiastically pointed out to him by the others, so that he can't stop smiling. It's becoming distressingly clear that Carl is a natural. He's totally in the zone. His focus on the game isn't distracted by panicked flights from the building, and he is unfazed when the group spends thirty minutes talking about highway accidents they've seen, instead of about Camille Paglia or *The Tale of Genji*.

I mutter the words, "Carl is my bête noir," but the very fact that I choose this term to describe the relationship is a good indication of why I need to choose it at all. Never mind, Loki may yet vanquish Thor; THRUSH could still make U.N.C.L.E. say uncle.

By the time my standard run comes around, I'm so conscious of time that I keep glancing up at the clock, which is just enough of a break in my concentration that I lose Dusty several times. At one point I find myself pivoting around on my heel like a music-box ballerina, trying to locate him. It's pretty much a calamity.

I return him to his crate; he creeps to the back and lowers himself onto his stomach with a sigh. I know how he feels; this entire day hasn't been much fun for either of us. And isn't fun supposed to be the whole point?

I stop at the vending machine to grab a Coke—though what I'm really craving is a vodka and tonic—and return to the standard course to watch my teammates run. As I arrive, Kim is on the line with KC. She starts off well enough but loses KC early and has to start calling her name to retrieve her. "KC, come! KC, come!"

I turn to where Carl is waiting in "the hole" (as they call the space just before the start gate), and just as it happened yesterday, the sound of Kim's voice immediately sets Fletcher off. "This is *eeeexcellent*," I hiss, all but stroking my fingers in anticipation of disaster.

Carl has increasing trouble keeping Fletcher in place. The dog wants to bolt, find his mom. I may leave this trial with nothing to

show for it but embarrassment and abashment, but so will my adversary. That will be some comfort. I begin to back away so that I
might gloat from the shadows, like Gollum.

And then I hear the note of real desperation in Carl's voice—
"Fletcher, c'mon, boy; Fletcher, *sit*"—and I think, "What the hell
is wrong with me?" This is an actual human being in actual distress
here, not some cartoon character in my head. And it occurs to me
that the manufacture of conflict where no conflict exists is a problem Dusty has as well. Again, have I been the source of it? Are the
pathologies I so lament in him the very ones I've bred in him by
my own behavior?

Time to put a stop to all that. After all, might I not have better
luck finding a place among these people if I stopped creatively visualizing myself as their nemesis? I walk up and say, "Hey there,
Fletcher! Hey there, boy!" and scratch his head, immediately
drawing his attention away from Kim, whose shouts are still all
too audible from the ring. "Hey, Fletcher," I say, making my voice
shrill and fluty. "Hey, guess what? Fourscore and seven years ago
our forefathers brought forth a new nation, conceived in liberty
and *someone's in the kitchen with Diiiinah*"—switching to a falsetto
croon to keep him off-guard—"*someone's in the kitchen I know-whoa-
whoa-whoa . . .*"

I'm up to *fee-fi-fiddley-eye-oh* by the time Carl is called out to
the start line, and between us we've managed to divert Fletcher's
attention from Kim. He shoots me a quick "Thanks" as he heads
into the ring.

I join the All Fours team members on the sidelines and take a
seat next to another excellent competitor, Alise, a willowy blond
who smiles and starts making small talk; but she keeps one eye on

the start, where Carl has just put Fletcher in a sit-stay. He then turns and walks out past the first jump, past the second jump, and then turns back to give Fletcher the command to go.

Alise stops in midsentence and coos admiringly, "That is a *sexy* lead out!"

Sexy it may be, but it almost ruins the run: Fletcher dips around the first jump and Carl has to double back and get him over it, so there's a refusal right off the bat. But give the man credit: he gets his dog in hand and takes him through the course pretty much flawlessly. And in damn good time.

Carl and Fletcher have Q'd.

Carl's beaming with well-earned pride when he bursts through the gate and is immediately met with—if not outright buffeted by—congratulations. "Nice run, great job," I blurt before I'm shunted aside by other admirers. And as I retreat, I think with some satisfaction, "I had a bit of a hand in that."

"Well, boy," I say to Dusty as we drive home, our first trial now behind us, "what have we learned this weekend?" In the rear-view mirror I can see his ears pivot attentively, but he offers no response. I'm disappointed, but what did I expect, for my dog to sum up the life-lessons I'd taught him?

Something inside me sloshes, and I feel a sudden sharp pressure against the walls of my bladder.

"What we've learned," I tell him, suddenly snarling, "is always to use the men's room *before* getting on the goddamn interstate."

CHAPTER 9

Doubt and Distraction

It's almost a month before our second trial. I can never seem to remember that you have to apply for these things well in advance, and what with the growing popularity of the sport, slots tend to fill in pretty quickly and latecomers like me are shut out. It seems to me that future champions shouldn't have to bother with tedious paperwork, but apparently the rest of the world begs to differ. All right then. I've managed to squeak us on to the rolls of an outdoor trial held in Belvidere, Illinois, a place whose name I've never heard mentioned in all my years of living in this area. It must be one of those spots on the map in a point-size you need to be a fruit fly to read.

The day arrives and the CD I've chosen for the trip is Ravel's *Daphnis et Chloé* suites performed by the London Symphony Orchestra with André Previn conducting. It's heady stuff, exotic and undulating, though it ends up reminding me of *Star Trek*. I muse a bit on the way rhythms and melodies of this kind are still being used to illustrate the lives of mythical constructs—except that the myths have shifted from shepherds and pirates to starship captains. I'm just wondering whether the occasional appearance of togalike costumes or Hellenic architecture in mid-sixties science fiction is a subconscious reflex or a conscious tribute to the genre's forbears, when it occurs to me that if any of my agility colleagues knew this was how I spent my time they'd think I was stone crazy.

We reach the trial site—the Boone County Fairgrounds—and park on the lawn, then go to seek out the rest of the All Fours team. It's a fine autumn day. The air is crisp but the sun just warm enough to counter it. Really the perfect weather for competing under an open sky.

There are, as usual, two courses set up—one for standard, another for jumpers—and the excellent dogs are already running. We circle the perimeter of both rings, Dusty lagging behind because he's riveted by the fascinating aromas of so many passing rumps. I don't see a single familiar face. It occurs to me that even though a lot of the members of the All Fours crew are hardcore agility folk, they don't necessarily go to every single trial. And that if I want the benefit of their company at a given event, I should probably ask in advance if they plan on going.

I'm just resigning myself to a weekend spent on my own—and a corresponding relief, somewhat shameful, that at least I won't have to attempt small talk—when I spot Gus, of Gus and Deb, one of the other agility couples in the All Fours ranks. He's slouched deep in a folding chair, fast asleep. There's an empty chair next to his, which can only be Deb's. I stand dithering for a minute, uncertain of what to do. I could wake him, of course, but that'd be a tad rude. Plus, what do I say after the initial, "Hey, Gus, how's it going?" My eternal problem: the conversational freeze-up.

With Deb this will not be an issue, as she's one of those people who seem able to keep up a steady stream of conversation with anyone who might happen to be within a dozen yards. Or thirty. Or a hundred. It's a trait a lot of Italian women possess, and that a lot of Italian men don't—probably for that reason. Growing up among them, I've learned to marvel at the lives of these women, which all seem to follow the same unvarying arc: demure and virginal in girlhood, shy and smiling as brides, and then accruing more and more presence and power with age—even becoming physically larger, until they actually seem to swallow up the men in whose shadows they once meekly stood. Italian men suffer the inverse: growing taciturn and leaner, even spectral, with age.

Gus, however, has escaped this fate; he hasn't diminished at all. Both he and Deb are substantial people, and ranged around their chairs today are coolers, hampers, bags of goodies—a real bounty. They're very generous with it too, in the time-honored Italian way, always offering up a handful of this or a paper plate of that. They're a very likable pair, but I've always felt a little intimidated around them; this is, after all, a couple who have really sat down and made some choices, and everything about them broadcasts confidence in the results. They're a team, a unit, a bulwark of certainty. They even dress alike, in complementing windbreakers. Whereas here I am, all by my lonesome, plagued by the moral relativism of this modern era that makes it so difficult to commit wholly to any decision at all. Should I even be here today, amusing myself by cavorting under the open sky, when the rain forest is disappearing and AIDS is sweeping across Africa?

I look down at Dusty, who's quivering with anxiety. It's no wonder he's a neurotic mess; I must still be infecting him with my aura. I try to shake off the languor and doubt—literally so; I jiggle my arms in the air and shake my legs, then set off on a brisk walk to steady our nerves.

We head away from the trial ground and across a broad lawn that gently slopes downward and then up again, as though God just got up from a nap and left his elbow imprinted here. Dusty sniffs contentedly, and I let him follow the scent—allow him, in other words, to lead me, a rare privilege, since in the crowded, perilous city it's vital that I be the one guiding his steps.

Eventually he looks up at me and blinks, as though he'd temporarily forgotten my existence. The smells here must be deeply engrossing reading for him. I look over my shoulder and am momentarily surprised at how far we've meandered. The trial site is just a barnacle clinging tenuously to horizon line. An occasional whistle is the only sound to break through the cloaking buzz of the surrounding insects—nature's white noise. I feel a little thrill of pleasure at being so far removed from any other sentient soul. It's bracing, this sudden shower of solitude, after so many months of life in the city, where it seems there's always somebody pressing against you from one angle or another.

I used to enjoy this privilege fairly frequently, back when Jeffrey's mom was alive. We'd drive out to see her—just a dozen miles or so from this very spot—and while Jeffrey went on into the house to greet her, I'd take the dog to stretch her legs after the long car ride. Together we'd walk to the very perimeter of the orchard on the property, where I could be reasonably certain I was the only human being within a quarter-mile radius. It was exhilarating; it felt like I was getting away with something—opting, for a few clandestine moments, out of the entire human race.

Dusty's eyelids are nearing half-mast. He seems to have entered some kind of fugue state. He continues to trot along, nose to the ground, but there's no purpose in it now—it's a Zen thing, if a dog has the capacity for Zen. Looking at him now, I'm tempted to say that dogs *are* Zen, that they embody the principle at its purest—that kind of oneness with everything, a quiet melding of the self into the great harmony of being. Of course I'm deliberately ignoring any inconvenient memories of him yapping wildly out the window or hurling himself at FedEx trucks.

His equilibrium seems restored, so I gently tug his leash to steer him back the way we came. I still have to check in, get my armband, and pick up the maps of the courses we'll be running. Dusty emits a little huff, as though reading my mind. But he follows me all the same.

After checking in we come upon Deb, who's just parting from another acquaintance so that she doesn't even have to take a breath between conversations. "Hi, Rob, I didn't know you were gonna be here today. It's beautiful out, isn't it? What are you running in today, still novice? Don't feel bad—Becky's been in novice for six years. Did you see Gus? Are you thirsty? No, no one else is here; they're all at Fort Wayne. You didn't know about Fort Wayne? I thought everyone knew about Fort Wayne. Me and Gus stayed here because we think maybe we'll get a chance to take the boat out, not too many weekends left for that. We're staying at a bed-and-breakfast tonight. Gus, wake up. Rob's here." We've reached their small encampment, and Deb shakes his shoulder. He sputters awake.

"Hey, Rob, how ya doin'?" he says. "Want a Coke or somethin'?"

Their accents are genuine South Side Chicago, and are like music to me out here on the rural frontier. "Where are the girls?" I ask, referring to their cocker spaniels, Becky, Bridget, Brittany, and Brandy. I've trained with all of them for a number of years and I still can't tell them apart, a fact I do my best to hide from Deb and Gus. After all, I know how irked I get when someone can't tell the difference between Dusty and Carmen (to me they barely look like the same species, much less the same breed). Thus whenever one of the four steps up onto my thigh to say hello, I always respond with an all-purpose, "Hey there, sweetheart!"

"They're in their crates," Deb says.

"Oh, I've still got to set up mine," I say. "Which one of these buildings is the crating area?"

She tosses her head in the direction of one of the long, flat outbuildings and says, "That one, I think; I'm not sure 'cause we're just keeping the girls in the van." I turn to see the van in question, parked next to a tree with its back door hanging open for circulation, and am a bit surprised that Gus has parked so close to the rings. I ask Deb about this, and she hints that they know someone who gave them a nod. I don't recognize the name, and feel again like I'm on the outside of some vast agility fraternity—a dilettante, a dabbler.

Still, my Saab 9-3 isn't quite as accommodating for a crate—the only way I can fit one in at all is to fold it up first—plus I'd be too nervous to leave the door hanging open. The odds of anyone stealing my stereo way out here, east of Eden, are remote at best, but what can I say. Living in the city all these years has left me more than a little paranoid. Well, paranoia is good on the mean streets; it's what helps you survive.

And yet Gus and Deb are Chicagoans too. I try not to draw any deflating inferences. Possibly it's just one more example of strength in numbers: as a couple, they can pool their self-assurance in a way I really can't. I try to imagine being out here with Jeffrey. He would absolutely, no question about it, pull up as close to the trial site as possible; hell, given half a chance he'd park under the A-frame. Of course he'd do that even without me. Maybe I'm the only one who's suffering a self-assurance deficit here. I'm always minding the rules and doing what I'm told, no matter how it chafes. Actually, more often than not it *doesn't* chafe, as if my will has been permanently whittled down.

I remind myself that the whole point of this agility adventure is to shake off that shroud of timorousness and restraint. To be bold, to be heroic, to strive and achieve. I need it, Dusty needs it—it's high time we went out there and just *did* it.

First, however, I need to sit down and examine the novice standard course. It seems a rather puny segue from my big rhetorical exhortation, but as Alexander or Caesar certainly knew, every great victory hinges on a series of small maneuvers.

Which in this case seem to begin with a front cross after the tire—something I'm almost positive Alexander and Caesar never had to pull off.

The front cross ends up going beautifully. Unfortunately, I follow by leading Dusty to the wrong obstacle, which officially constitutes an off course—my bad, not his—after which I grow nervous about making another mistake, and of course transmit that nervousness directly to him, as if by laser beam. I stop short, he stops short; I start second-guessing him, he starts giving up on me. At one point he even sits down. Just plonks his butt right in the middle of the field. I feel like joining him.

Deb is there at the end with kind words and an ice-cold Coke, but I'm not to be placated; I have to steel myself against panic for my next run, jumpers with weaves. While I'm putting Dusty back in his crate, someone comes up—tall guy, glasses, salt-and-pepper beard—and introduces himself as Jim. He has Shelties too, he says, and knows how skittish they can be in the ring. As if to provide exhibit A, he reaches down to stroke Dusty, who responds by backing to the farthest corner of the crate and hiding his head under his shank.

"Have you tried lavender oil?" he asks.

I blink. The question seems to have been reeled in from some other conversation. "I . . . don't think I have," I say, uncertain of his meaning. Is this some inquiry into my personal hygiene? I give myself a surreptitious sniff.

"It really calms them down," he says, nodding toward the crate. I'm just wondering what it would take to get Dusty to ingest lavender oil when Jim adds, "You rub a little behind their ears just before you go in the ring. It's a very soothing aroma."

"Ah," I say. And I can't think of anything to add. I'm having too much trouble with the idea of going all airy-fairy-herbal on a dog. I mean, the happiest I've ever seen my pack was after they'd managed to roll themselves filthy in deer shit. *That's* the scent that made them feel contented and complete. It took over an hour to bathe the skin-blistering, Agent Orange–like stench out of them and they were sullen and resentful every single second of it. In view of which, I seriously doubt a few polite daubs of flowery foo-faraw would do anything but annoy a real canine.

"You're here tomorrow?" Jim asks, completely unperturbed by how antisocial both my dog and I are being. "I'll bring you some."

"That's very generous," I say, "but really you don't have to do that. I can pick it up myself. Do I find it at a pharmacy or . . . ?"

He waves dismissively as he turns on his heels. "It's no big deal, I've got plenty. See you then."

He's gone before I can think to thank him. God damn this urban-cynic wariness that makes me suspicious of anyone who approaches me unbidden. "What the hell does he want from me?" is my reflexive reaction. And I hate to admit it, but there's part of me that's half-convinced the guy will show up tomorrow, slip me a vial of some cheap gunk, and then demand fifty bucks for it.

But I've got to remember that I'm not in the city. I'm out here on the prairie where honest, decent, God-fearin' folk help a body out, whether it's with the hayin' or the reapin' or his agility dog's nervous complaint.

Some lavender oil can only have improved our jumpers run, which devolves rapidly into a circus. Dusty has a clutch of refusals, and we end up straggling off the course, gasping, after seventy-seven seconds. The allowed course time is forty-one. We were more than thirty seconds over. I'd gone out there striving for an epochal run and succeeded only in that an epoch is about how long it took. I'm surprised we weren't whistled off the course. Then someone at the gate tells me we were—I just didn't hear it and kept going. A real festival of humiliation I've got on my hands here.

And the weekend's only half over.

CHAPTER 10

From the Jaws of Defeat

After a performance like that, all you can really do is skulk out of town. Which we do. Straight back to the city, where hordes of people are out in the gorgeous weather, biking and picnicking and grilling burgers in the park, and jamming up traffic something awful.

We're on Lawrence Avenue, about three-quarters of a mile from our block, and traffic is just . . . Not. Moving. Ninety minutes I've driven —close enough to home to stumble there blindfolded— only to be stopped in my tracks by the great human comedy unfolding before me.

And just when I think my nerves have been shredded as completely as they can be, I hear an awful sound from the backseat. A kind of muffled gastric rumbling: *mmm-glrp, mmm-glrp, mmm-glrp* . . .

I whirl around and find Dusty with a hideous grin on his face, his head bobbing like a pigeon's. *Mmm-glrp, mmm-glrp——*

"No . . . no! Hold on, boy," I say desperately. "We're *almost* home—just calm down, *please*."

But of course he's far beyond the reach of any blandishments I might fire at him. A moment later he projects a really quite impressive amount of vomit all over my leather interior.

"Oh, God," I say, craning my neck to survey the damage. The hothead in the Chevy Impala behind me lays on his horn. I turn back to find that traffic has crept up a good yard and a half; apparently the Impala guy is afraid someone might cut in front of me and claim it. Possibly someone on a tricycle or a pogo stick. I don't know and don't care. I've got bigger problems.

A few minutes later, we reach a corner that hosts a gas station. I pull in and retrieve from the trunk one of the towels I keep on hand for such emergencies. When I open the back door, the vomit oozes out like lava. It's really a startling amount; how can so small a dog have had this much bile in him? Dusty looks guiltily up at me, his head hung low. "Don't worry, boy," I say; "it could happen to anybody. Nothing to be ashamed of. Have it cleaned up in no time."

But cleanup is actually more challenging than that. The offending substance is just viscous enough to resist absorption by the towel yet liquid enough to seep into every nook and cranny, with rivulets running under the seat beyond the reach of my hand. I throw in the towel (or rather, throw *out* the towel) after managing to clear away the worst, by which time my head is pounding and the sun dipping low in the sky.

I give Dusty an absolving scratch under the chin, get back behind the wheel, and pull into traffic—with some difficulty because no one wants to readmit me. In fact when I do succeed, it's only by daring to cut off someone on the assumption that her car means more to her than mine to me (since hers is a brand-new BMW and most likely vomit free). She brakes hard and then curses me out— I can read her lips in the rearview mirror. "Geez, lady," I mutter. "You kiss your mama with that mouth?"

Traffic picks up a bit, and we make up the rest of the distance in only a matter of minutes. As I turn into the alley that leads to our garage, I feel physically lighter, as if I've come through a gauntlet relatively unscathed. Finally, we arrive. I depress the garage opener, and as the door slowly rises, I hear again from the backseat, *mmm-glrp*, *mmm-glrp*.

"No, Dusty. *No!* We're here! We're *here!*"

And so we are. But for the second time today, thirty seconds too late.

"I'm thinking of not going back tomorrow," I say to Jeff over dinner.

"Mm," he says, unimpressed. When he's swallowed his last forkful of chicken marsala, he reminds me, "Your crate's still there."

"They can have it. I'll buy a new one."

He shrugs and says, "Your call," then starts to clear away the dishes.

"I mean it," I tell him. "Today was brutal. I don't see any point in repeating it."

"Fine," he says. "You want dessert?"

"No, thanks." I give him a piercing look. "You think I'm being juvenile."

"No," he says as he fetches a tub of ice cream from the freezer. "Actually, it's a sign of maturity to forgo dessert."

I clench my teeth. "You know what I meant."

He plunks two scoops of *dulce de leche* into a bowl. "If you say so."

"You think I'm being adolescent. A crybaby. Giving up."

"*Someone* seems to be saying that, but it doesn't appear to be me."

"I know what I'm doing. I'm a grown man, at least allow me that."

"No one's saying otherwise." He holds up the tub before replacing it in the freezer. "Last chance. Sure you don't want any?"

I shake my head. "I'm a grown man and I know my own mind. I don't make decisions lightly. I make them in the fullness of intent, and they *mean* something."

He brings the bowl to the table. "I'm not arguing." He tucks into the ice cream.

I watch him enjoying it for almost nine whole seconds, then reach over and say, "I'll just have one bite . . ."

It's windy the next day in Belvidere—so windy that dogs are being blown right off the dog walk. In fact while I'm watching, one tiny Yorkie looks like he's going to be carried clear off the fairgrounds—the wind just picks him up and away he goes. I admit it, I laugh; I'm a terrible human being.

As I do my walk-through, I'm strategically numb. Yesterday's military approach, breaking down the run into a series of achievable objectives, fell decisively flat. And with the wind being what it is, I figure the best I can do is just get through this, learn what I can from whatever mistakes I make, and then try to figure out some other scheme for getting Dusty through a course without disgrace or dishonor.

The bars are being raised to sixteen inches. Our cue. I go and fetch Dusty from the crating center, where the wind is strumming the tin walls like a washboard. Dusty comes out blinking and jittery, as though the noise has badly jangled his nerves. Terrific, just what I need: a Sheltie with posttraumatic stress disorder

I repeat to myself, "Just get through it. Just get through it. Just get through it."

We're on the line. I put Dusty in a sit-stay and walk out toward the first obstacle. I look to the timekeeper; he nods, "When you're ready."

I turn to Dusty. "Come," I tell him. He hops up and moves toward me; I lash out my arm and say, "Tunnel!"

He disappears into the entry and I move along the U-shaped length, talking him through it so he doesn't panic and turn back. He pops out the opposite end and I immediately shout, "Over!" gesturing him toward two successive jumps directly in front of us. "Over, boy!" He clears both.

Weaves are next. They're on our left, not his best approach to this particular obstacle, but there's not enough time to get him on the right, so we plow ahead. And he botches his entry. But it's okay; you're allowed that in novice. I get him back in correctly and he threads himself through the six bars nicely. It may help that the wind's at his booty, bustling him along. I get on his right for the next several jumps, which form a big semicircle: "Over! Over! Over! Over!" Then another front cross, to get back on the left for the last three jumps—and then that's it, we're past the finish line and off the course, and I'm retrieving Dusty's leash and snapping it back around his collar, and people keep smiling at us and saying strange things like "nice job" and "well done."

What? What just happened?

"That was *beautiful*," says Deb when I swing by her and Gus's chairs (still in the same spot—they seem utterly impervious to the squall kicking up all around them).

"You think we've Q'd?" I ask, slightly out of breath.

"Oh, yeah, for sure," she says. "I think you've *placed*."

To my utter shock, we have. Dusty has ranked second among the sixteen-inchers. We get a big red ribbon with our names on it and the date and the place and the score (for future generations, who will surely want to know).

I'm on my way back to the crating area when I'm hailed by Jim, who says he's been looking for me. He takes my hand and places a little vial of lavender oil in it. "You'll see," he says. "It really calms 'em down."

I thank him, trying not to let "too late—don't need it" shine too baldly from my face, promising to apply it in an hour or so when we have our standard run.

Lavender oil notwithstanding, that run doesn't go so well. Dusty does a Peter Pan off the dog walk, due, I think, more to ill will than ill wind.

But it doesn't matter. It can't erase the fact that we've picked up a leg on the way to our first title. A fact that is still sinking in. We've done what we came to do. We've Q'd. I feel exultant—like there should be a ticker-tape parade in our honor, dancing girls, a presentation from the mayor, a guest slot on *Conan* or *Leno*.

But of course there's none of that. Only the two of us, Dusty and me, staring at each other in the dull roar of the wind. Well, fine. That's what champions are when you get down to it. Solitary creatures. Self-contained. Content to savor their victories in manly, Spartan solitu—

"Hey, Rob!"

I turn. Deb and Gus are a few yards off, big grins on their faces, a quartet of leashes trailing behind them with a wind-streaked cocker at the end of each one.

"Congratulations again," says Deb. "That was a really beautiful run!"

My face burns with pride and I try to thank her, but what actually issues from my lips is something like, "Ish, vllmik." She waves, then she and Gus turn and head toward their van.

Recognition from a colleague! So that's what it's like. I replay the moment in my head, even as I'm living it. This is a taste of how it feels to *belong*.

CHAPTER 11

Tales from the Cryptic

Another competition, a week later. Despite entering late, I've landed a spot in the Great Lakes Belgian Tervuren Club trial in Manhattan, Illinois. Fortunately, it's another gorgeous, buttery day—temperature in the seventies, the sun splashing indiscriminately over everything. Good day to be alive.

Of course I'd be feeling that even if there were a monsoon. After all, I've got momentum now. Our first qualifying score was just six days ago. It's like we've taken a little pause for breath, now we're ready for our next triumph. Even Dusty seems calmer and more confident today. I've lowered the window a bit, just enough for him to stick his snout out, and he's seriously grooving on the scents. I can't imagine what there is to smell out there, beyond exhaust fumes and distressed rubber, but he's all over it.

I've made a serious miscalculation with this weekend's orchestral selection, however. Mahler's Symphony no. 4—what was I thinking? Far too spiritual, too ethereal, with doubt and uncertainty rumbling just below the surface. Not at all my mood today.

I'm feeling very much flesh and blood, thank you, and want nothing more than to line up all the world's obstacles and knock them down one by one. Handel's *Fireworks Music* would've been better. Or some bombastic overture by John Williams. I mean, if it's going to sound like a film score anyway.

I'm also buoyed by a week's worth of kudos from my All Fours cohorts. As is the custom, I sent our Yahoo! group a "brags" e-mail about Dusty's second-place finish and was immediately inundated with a wave of effusive congratulations. Everyone seems to have taken the time to drop a line. There was no Yahoo! group—no Yahoo! for that matter—back when I competed in trials with Carmen, so I never realized how tightly knit and supportive a team of colleagues can be. I'm not sure how I'd define "community," but I know it when I'm in it, and this week I've been wallowing in it.

Surprisingly, the attention isn't just gratifying: it's also humbling. I realize now how much this kind of approbation means, and I'm ashamed at how stingy I've been with it all these months—never responding to any of the "brags" e-mails that have landed in my own in-box. I resolve always to do so from now on, even if it's just two or three words—"Well done!" or "Attapooch!" It's becoming clearer to me that acceptance isn't something you wait for—it's something you actively claim. And more importantly, something you *give*.

Landmarks grow sparser as we near the trial site. If I thought Belvidere was the end of the earth, it's only because I hadn't yet seen Manhattan. This is rural in a way I've never really encountered before. There are stretches of road where I might easily be in the eighteenth century. I start to keep an eye out for highwaymen and cutthroats.

When I finally reach the Rush 'N' Around Agility Center, I can see that it's really just a big prefabricated structure—a pole barn more or less—surrounded by several acres of not very much. Dogs are leaping and careening and bellowing everywhere. Dusty gets out of the car, has one look at the pandemonium, and tries to get back in again.

The first thing we do is take in the lay of the land. In short order we learn that the standard ring is in the barn and the jumpers ring outside. Strangely, there's a third ring as well. We get close enough to determine that it's running an entirely new class, called FAST. I've never heard of it before, and the course looks strange to me—the numbering system on the obstacles makes no sense. On a standard or jumpers course, you start at the cone numbered one, proceed to two, then three, and so on. Here, there are about seven different obstacles all numbered one. And each new contestant seems to be running in a different pattern.

Well, it needn't concern us, we're not registered for it, and with a name like FAST it's unlikely I'll be signing Dusty up anytime soon. We'd be better off waiting for a class called "leisurely."

Dusty's still acting fidgety, so I take him on a walk to calm his nerves. We cover a good third of a mile before I tug on his leash to turn him back. He seems much more relaxed, but now I'm the one who's feeling jittery. The sheer emptiness of this place unsettles me a little. It's one thing to bask in isolation from other human beings; it's quite another to have the weight of the entire cosmos crushing down on you, with nowhere to hide.

As we head back, I can't help taking in the vastness of the vistas that surround me—a majestic sweep of creation, notched here and there by cows, horses, silos, tractors. Living in the city, you forget what it's like to see distances, to espy something on the far, far horizon. You forget your eyes can actually *work* that way, that this manner of seeing the world is available to you. It's the reason Venetian artists were behind the rise of landscape painting: they grew up in a place with no landscapes at all, so when they got to the mainland and saw them stretching out in all directions, their natural reaction was, "Hoo boy, I'm-a gonna paint me summa that!" I feel a similar impulse now, but all I can do is take a picture with my cell phone. Hardly the ideal medium for conveying this kind of immensity.

Back at the site, I set Dusty's crate beneath a birch tree with riotously colored leaves, then go to check in. Once I've got my armband and course maps, I head back to the car. I've got about an hour before my standard run, and I can use the time to mount another attack on the dried vomit in the backseat. I've been at this job all week, with diminishing success. There are certain crevasses and gullies I can't adequately reach, and the stuff has virtually calcified in there. I do what I can, chipping away, but it's increasingly clear that I'll never get it all, try as I might. If it weren't so visible, I wouldn't mind so much. I knew glory came at a price, but did it have to be my resale value?

I go back to the barn to check on where things stand. The open class has wound up, and the volunteers are refitting the course for novice. The call sheet is up, and I put a check by my name to indicate that I'm here. As I skim the list, I recognize one of today's other competitors: Vicky Bruning. She's the breeder from whom Jeffrey and I bought our very first dog, Nelson, some eighteen years ago. According to the sheet, she's here to run a Sheltie in the twelve-inch category.

I met her only that one time, and very long ago it was, so I have no recollection of what she looks like. I scope out all the women of a certain age with Shelties, but of course this is an agility trial so there's a whole glee club of those, and I'm not prepared to approach each of them and ask, "Pardon me, might you be Vicky?" I don't have a lot to say to the real Vicky, so I can't expend that much social energy on red herrings.

But as I seek her out, I find myself remembering Nelson. He was very good company, and he got plenty of opportunities to be. Back then, Jeffrey and I were much more active and on the go, and whenever we dashed off somewhere we took him along. It's no wonder he never suffered from the kind of restlessness that Carmen endured when we adopted her years later, after middle age had slowed us down. Fortunately, by then there was agility to take up the slack. Apparently, Vicky Bruning has discovered this as well.

As I go looking for her, it suddenly strikes me as odd that I'm actively seeking out company. When I first learned I'd be the only All Fours team member to compete at this event, I'd felt a little thrill of relief at the idea of being alone. But now that I'm here, I feel the need to connect. Is it possible I'm becoming one of these people? Looking around me, I can't believe this is true. I'm the only one on site who isn't wearing dog-themed apparel; the only one who didn't arrive in a van plastered with canine decals. I can't imagine what it would take for me to put on a "Sheltie Spin Doctor" T-shirt, or to slap my Saab with a bright yellow "Agility Dog On Board" sticker. What I'm feeling is obviously some kind of fluke, probably weather related. But I go with it.

I don't actually locate Vicky till the walk-through. There are only twenty-four people in the entire novice class, so it's just a matter of honing in on the ones who are about the right age, then checking the names on their armbands. Even so, this is a little difficult with all two-dozen handlers marching in various patterns around me; it's like trying to count supersized baby chicks. Eventually, I ferret her out; she's older than I remember (well, nearly two decades *have* passed) and has that unself-conscious look many dog people maintain, like they've dressed themselves in whatever clothes were closest at hand, regardless of how anything works with anything else—which is usually not at all. Her hair is thin and a bit wild, and as she strides the course purposefully, her face wears a look that is somehow both distracted and highly focused. An odd bird, to be sure, but again—she's a breeder. They tend to be rather singular people.

I approach her a while later, while we're both waiting for our turns to run. "Vicky? My name's Robert Rodi. I don't know if you remember me; I bought a dog from you eighteen years ago. Nelson . . . ?"

She gives me a briefly hooded look, as though filing through some internal database, then brightens and says, "Oh, certainly, I remember Nelson." For a moment I think she's going to ask after him, but of course she'd know he must be dead by now. And being a breeder she won't be sentimental enough to care how. She nods at Dusty, who's all but hiding behind my legs, and says, "This is your dog now?"

"One of them," I say, and I gently pull him out from behind me. "This is Dusty. And that's your Dakota, right? She's beautiful. Dusty, say hi to Dakota." Dusty refuses, but Dakota takes the initiative and steps up to give him a polite sniff—and seeing this silky, bouncy, unrelentingly adorable specimen side by side with

Dusty, I'm reminded again of how funny looking he is, how scrawny and gangly and pinched. And for a moment, God forgive me, I am embarrassed.

"He's a cryptic blue," I say proudly, grasping for the one incontestable arrow in his quiver.

"I know," she says darkly. "I'm seeing more and more of those lately." She shakes her head. "Irresponsible breeding." She must see the stricken look on my face, because she quickly adds, "Well, *he's* not irresponsible."

The world has suddenly turned upside down. The very quality I've been accustomed to thinking most to Dusty's credit is suddenly presented to me as a kind of shame from which he needs to be absolved of blame. Suddenly Dakota backs away from us, as though recognizing that we're from the wrong side of the genetic tracks.

While I stand here, reeling, Vicky continues in a manner-of-fact way to rebuke the practices of the kind of reckless Sheltie breeders who strive to create new strains for variety's sake. "The pure whites are the most tragic," she says. "They don't usually live long." She gives Dusty another look, as if to ask, "And how old is this one, anyway?"

"That's terrible," I say, I hope not too defiantly, "but really Dusty's in terrific health."

Again I expect her to offer some kind of token compliment—everybody does this—just some little reference to how handsome or smart or friendly he is, and you don't even have to *mean* it, but she seems oblivious to this kind of nicety. I suppose I should expect that. After all, Shelties are livestock to her.

All the same, I feel suddenly stupid and rudderless. I don't know what to do or say, so I start looking for the first opportunity to escape. Fortunately, at just this moment the twenty-inch dogs finish running and the bar goes down to sixteen. I excuse myself from Vicky and go wait in the hole.

Maybe because of this little disorienting moment, our standard run is not a success. Dusty bails off both the teeter and the dog walk, and as tempting as it'd be to go back and retry them, that's not allowed for contact obstacles the way it is for jumps and weaves. If you try it, you'll be whistled off the course. So we're forced to finish off the balance of our run while knowing that there's no hope of qualifying.

Of course Vicky has witnessed this whole pitiable performance. And of course Vicky and Dakota then go on to Q easily.

For some reason, Vicky is competing in standard only, not in jumpers, so she now collects her coat and crate and departs. "I'm sure we'll run into each other again," she says as she goes, and I'm left wondering if I can possibly get another dog before that happens.

By now it's lunchtime, and the agility club is serving up some kind of shredded-beef sandwiches to the volunteer workers. The beef is in a big steaming vat, and the smell of it begins to make me queasy. When people start glooping it up onto spongy white buns, I can feel my gorge rise.

I've learned not to make too big a display of my food snobbery, because it doesn't go over very well. People tend not to like it when you imply that they've spent pretty much their entire lives going about a fundamental human activity in completely the wrong way. They get their backs up. Still, not commenting on the offense doesn't mean I have to endure it, so I go back to the car and fetch my own lunch: a bowl of tortellini *al pesto*, made with the last of this summer's basil crop. I eat it seated beneath a tree, Dusty beside me, watching the conclusion of the open jumpers class.

Ironically, our own jumpers run turns out to be a winner. It feels great as we're running it, and we even earn some applause as we finish. When the scores go up, I see to my astonishment that not only have we Q'd, we've also taken first place: we're going home with a blue ribbon! Granted, there were only two dogs in the sixteen-inch category, and the other one was a bit of a spaz, so it's not *that* great a victory—but what the hell, we'll take it.

There's no denying it: we're on a roll. The national championships just got a little bit closer. They're held in March, in Tulsa. It's not too soon to check on air fares; we might get a deal by booking this early.

I pick up our ribbon and head to the car. Dusty walks beside me with swagger bordering on arrogance. I feel compelled to take him down a peg. "Why couldn't you have done that when Vicky Bruning was watching?" I ask. "Just to show her you're not some twitching experiment by Dr. Mengele?" It's no use. I can't even dim his pride. He's a little hero, and he knows it.

CHAPTER 12

Friends and Neighbors

The next night our friends Annie and Kevin have us over to dinner. He's an architect; she's an archivist. He's tall, carrot topped, bespectacled, a sly wit who's quick with a quip, while she's, well, pretty much the same (though admittedly more strawberry brunette than redhead). They're one of the more perfectly matched couples I've ever met; they seem to have emerged from the same pod—and then carried the pod away with them. Their house is warm and spacious and is choked with paintings, found objects, and endearing bits of kitsch. They're the parents we all wish we'd had. They have no children, which is probably the secret.

Annie has cooked up an enormous pork roast—by the looks of it, all the butcher did was remove the legs, ears, and tail—and after an extended cocktail hour, we've at last sat down to eat it. Bottles of wine are opened and mashed sweet potatoes brought to the table, singing of ginger. A crisp green salad with fennel and citrus is set before me, completing the aromatic logjam. I feel completely contented.

Inevitably, the conversation turns to my endeavors with Dusty. "Oh, we're doing very well," I say. "We're only on our third trial, and we've already racked up two legs toward a title."

"How many legs do you need?" Annie asks.

"For tap dancing, two," says Kevin. "Hopscotch, one."

"Sack racing, four," adds Jeffrey.

"*Three*," I say, retaking control of the conversation. "If he gets three qualifying scores in this particular class, he gets his novice title in jumpers with weaves."

"Is that like jumping with hair extensions?"

I ignore this and forge ahead. "Then he moves up to what's called the open class, and if he gets three qualifying scores there—"

"It's open and shut."

Everyone cackles, and I feel a sting of irritation that the people closest to me aren't taking this entirely seriously. But the idea of saying so—of delivering or even implying some kind of rebuke—is inconceivable. I'm at a dinner party, for God's sake. Suddenly, I realize that this must be an occupational hazard of belonging to two worlds. More than that, I have to admit to myself that I must actually, honestly belong to the agility world now, or I wouldn't be feeling the chafing of its incongruity with my everyday, urban one. It's a surprising epiphany.

Accordingly, I introduce a more self-deprecating subject: the downgrading of Dusty's previously revered cryptic blue status.

"So he's no longer Sheltie royalty?" Annie asks.

"Apparently not. More like a Sheltie eugenics victim."

"Oh, now, hold on," says Jeffrey, who's not only gotten over his initial aversion to Dusty but has become particularly fond of him. "You've got, what, the word of one snarky old lady?"

"A snarky old lady who breeds Shelties," I point out.

" 'Irresponsible breeding,' isn't that what she said? Those were her exact words, right?"

"More or less."

"Well, that's nothing but a value judgment. We're free to disagree, and I do. To me it's no more irresponsible than gardeners trying to breed different varieties of roses. Or trees that bear hybrid fruits."

"I think they do that by grafting the bark," says Kevin. "Hey, maybe that's how they get hybrid Shelties!"

Annie kicks him under the table, but so theatrically that we're all aware of it. "Well I don't care what anyone says, I think he's beautiful," she says consolingly. "I may change my mind if he ever lets me within the same zip code as him, but for now, I totally admire him from afar."

"You can admire him up close any time you like," I tell her. "Just come see him compete. You don't have to drive very far, not more than fifty miles or so really, and you'd be amazed by the way these dogs perform. It's . . ." I stop short, suddenly aware that I've gone a bit wild, trying to force my worlds to come together; it's harder than I thought, coexisting in two at once. Especially since emotionally I seem increasingly more invested in agility.

In the awkward silence that follows, Annie and Kevin's black cat, Squid, makes a kind of liquid entrance, moving slowly across the room in a series of glistening ripples. When she's gone, we find ourselves on the subject of cats. Now, I have nothing against cats; in fact I like them fine. But I don't find them a riveting subject for conversation. There just isn't that much to say about them. At least not compared to dogs: there's a basic experiential chasm between the two species. Dogs pull sleds, catch Frisbees, herd sheep, guard warehouses, sniff out explosives, lead the blind, retrieve game, and rescue lost hikers. They join the army, the police force, and the circus; they work on movie sets and in hospital wards. Whereas cats? Not big on leaving the house.

Then there's the whole matter of physical variations. Domestic cats remind me of the kind of suburban development where you get to choose from five or six house models, all of which are pretty much alike. Whereas with dogs, you've got a dizzying range of architecture: from statuesque Great Danes to teacup Pomeranians; sleek-coated Doberman pinschers to luxuriously maned Lhasa apsos; snub-nosed pugs to flute-snouted borzois; solid, squat bull terriers to elegantly long-limbed salukis. There's a dog to fit every aesthetic, from the aristocratic to the redneck. There's a size and shape to accommodate every habitat, from a bolt-hole to a palace. And there's a span of uncannily diverse facial variations not even the human species can match: Stare into the eyes of a Neapolitan mastiff, then into those of a cairn terrier: you're looking into very, very different worlds. And yet you're welcome there—you're always welcome.

But these are dear friends who have not only listened to me drone on about my dogs on more than one occasion but have done so with unfailing graciousness, and so I'm obliged to repay the favor with regard to their cats—who, admittedly, are amusing specimens, as cats go. The feline aptitude for playful murder is something I find particularly attractive; you just don't get that from canines.

I'm still pondering the differences between the two species when we return home to find our dogs all wound up about something happening somewhere on the street. We look out the window and can't see anything ourselves, but the way Dusty and Carmen are acting you'd think the Battle of Hastings was under way out there. Finally, the yapping and leaping and whining get to be too much for me. I open the back door and let them spill querulously out into the yard. They immediately start fence-running, barking and spinning in outrage at the presence of—what? We still don't know. Most likely we never will. Meantime, lights start flicking on in the apartment building next door, and a few wan faces peer down at us through the windows, exuding annoyance. I find myself thinking of Squid curled up atop a bookshelf, invulnerably contented and wholly self-contained and looking as though she just might decide not move a muscle for another eon or so. There are, I force myself to allow, as I corral my still-hysterical dogs and herd them back inside, some points to be made in favor of the cat.

It's late but I'm not tired, so I go and open my laptop and commence a good, solid hour of trawling the political Web sites, starting with the Drudge Report, Talking Points Memo, the Daily Kos, and the Huffington Post, then on to the various blogs on the *Atlantic*. It's a big election year and I'm becoming increasingly addicted to the drama of the coming primaries. At one point Jeffrey calls out from the kitchen, "I'm letting Dusty out again. He's acting all itchy." I murmur something noncommittal and continue reading.

Eventually, my eyes go all bleary and the words start to intermingle before me—a sure sign it's time to call it a night. I log off, then get up and douse the lights and drag myself to bed. My legs feel like they're made of lead.

The house is quiet; I seem to be the last one still up. I quickly strip down, leaving my clothes where they fall, and topple into bed; within seconds I'm dead to the world.

I'm roused by the doorbell, and by Carmen's howling response to it. I claw my way up from unconsciousness, lurch out of bed, and grab blindly for a robe. I connect with one, pull it off its hook, and try to don it while skittering down the staircase. I get the sleeves wrong and find myself wearing the thing backward, so that it flaps open behind me like a hospital gown. The doorbell rings again, signaling no small urgency, so I don't have time to fix it. I flip up the dead bolt, pausing only to wonder why Carmen's barking so furiously and Dusty not at all.

I swing open the door and there's a police officer on the welcome mat. Suddenly I'm *wide* awake. I reach behind me and try to pull the robe shut over my skinny white ass. "Hi," I say, a bit lamely. "Can I help you?"

It's too dark on the stoop to be sure, but I think he shoots me a patronizing look. "You got a dog?" he asks—which is a rather pointless question, as he surely heard Carmen yapping in response to the bell; what's more, she's chosen this moment to stick her nose out and take the intruder's scent. Do I have a dog? Hel-*looh*.

"Yes," I say, answering the question anyway, and I'm just about to introduce him to Carmen when I hear it: the unmistakable, if faint, sound of Dusty's shrill barking. But—where's it coming from?

Suddenly it all becomes clear. "Oh, crap," I say. "He's still out in the yard."

"That's right," says the officer.

"We forgot to bring him in."

"Mm-hmm."

"Someone called and complained?"

"Several someones."

"I'll go get him right now. Sorry, this really isn't like us; it's never happened before and I promise it'll never—" But he's already down the front steps, waving a hand in dismissal. He's got no more time for me; there are greater threats to public order to be dealt with tonight. I feel a sudden ecstasy of guilt that I'm responsible for diverting him from them. How many gang wars have now raged twenty minutes longer because I didn't lock up my nineteen-pound Sheltie?

From upstairs Jeffrey drowsily calls out, "What's going on?" I tell him not to worry and to go back to bed. I dash across the house—Carmen at my heels, yapping anew—and throw open the back door. I step out onto the deck and summon Dusty in from the yard in a hoarse but urgent stage whisper. He dutifully comes trotting on up, looking not at all abashed. In fact he seems infuriatingly pleased with himself, as though he's put in a fine night's work of warding off all manner of suspicious citizens, stray dogs, raccoons, possums, squirrels, falling leaves, old plastic bags, and whatever else might have had the temerity to bestir itself on his watch.

Taking a quick look up at the apartment building next door, I notice a few stray windows lit and scowling faces staring down at me. I'm utterly mortified, and not only because I look like an idiot, standing on the deck with my robe on backward, effectively mooning the moon, but also because I've become one of *those* people—the irresponsible, neglectful, contemptuous-of-their-fellow-man dog owners who plague every city neighborhood. How many nights have I lain awake, cursing some nearby householder for leaving his hound out all night to bay endlessly? It really is true: if we're not careful, we become the thing we hate.

Back inside I finally think to look at the clock: 3:18. I feel dizzy with guilt. Dusty must have been outside yapping for *hours* before my neighbors' innate civility was overwhelmed by sheer frustrated rage. I can't help wondering how many of them phoned in complaints— and *which* of them. It's going to be tough to show my face tomorrow. Jeffrey's lucky: he gets to slip away to his office in the early hours. I'm stuck here all day at the scene of the crime, as it were. Not that I expect any direct confrontations, just the inevitable daggers from accusing eyes, against which there is no real defense.

As it happens, my first encounter of the morning *is* a direct one. While walking the dogs I run into Bunny, one of our neighbors in the adjacent condominium building. She's on her way to work but stops to say hello to Carmen (who loves her)—then adds, a bit mischievously, "You left her out all night."

"Actually, that was Dusty," I say. It doesn't help that Dusty himself is now snarling at her as though he's never seen her before in his life.

"What happened?" she asks. Bunny's a friend, so the question is a fair one, but I just don't have an answer to it. I can't even say, "It was Jeffrey's fault," because everyone in the neighborhood knows the dogs are principally my responsibility.

I finally shrug and say, "We just forgot about him. I'm really sorry. If anyone else in the building mentions it, please pass along our apologies, and assure them it won't ever happen again."

She good-naturedly accepts my contrition, then after a few minutes of small talk continues on her way. Dusty gives one final, mighty dive in her direction as she goes, as if saying, "And don't come back!"

It's a wonder we have any friends on the block at all.

CHAPTER 13

A Glimmer of Glory

Weeks pass. We compete in a several more trials, but the third and final Q that will earn us our first title remains elusive. I've begun to wonder whether our earlier victories were flukes. Whether Dusty is in fact the canine equivalent of the ape left alone with a typewriter who will, given enough time, eventually bang out the complete works of Shakespeare. (Possibly starting with *Two Gentlemen of Verona*, which seems to me like a chimp already had a hand in writing it.)

But I refuse to give in to despair. And so today we're on our way to a novice-only trial in Spring Grove, Illinois, another town I've never even heard of. I always wonder about places like this. I mean, whence came the name Spring Grove? Is it in fact a grove? And was spring there such a rapturous floral idyll that the town council was compelled to make it their official brand, snubbing the family of some flinty Presbyterian founder who'd rather have had the place named after him? Was Spring Grove, in short, really that much more a Spring Grove than a Kinleyville or a Tuckerton?

Well if it ever was, it isn't now; these days it's just another depressing landscape of asphalt, strip malls, and drab little residential enclaves. Granted, the weather today is gray and rainy, the kind of day that can make Paris look Soviet.

Even more depressingly, MapQuest seems to have led me on a merry chase; the sudden turns and roundabouts required of me are almost vertiginous. Fortunately, the CD I've chosen for the drive is helping me keep sane: Dvořák's Symphony no. 7 in D Minor by the BBC Philharmonic, Vassily Sinaisky conducting. Although it's not the seventh itself that catches my fancy—it's too familiar, and in my view a bit too full of itself—but an extra piece on the program, *The Water Goblin*, to which I happily listen three times in succession. It's like a series of leitmotifs for agility; there are phrases that'd be perfect for the A-frame, the weave poles, even the table. If I were enough of a tech head to make movies of Dusty's runs on my laptop, this is definitely the soundtrack I'd use.

At last we arrive at the trial site: the WAG Building (WAG being the rather forced acronym of the Wisconsin-Illinois Agility Group), located in a glum little industrial park. This is by far the smallest agility facility I've yet seen. There's but a single ring, taking up perhaps three-quarters of the available interior. This means that when each class ends, the entire course will have to be taken down and rebuilt, vastly adding to the trial's running time. In my naïveté, I'd thought today's event would make for a quick morning because it's limited to novice competitors. Now I'm getting the first inklings that I might be here well into the afternoon.

The cramped crating area is piled high, dogs stacked on top of dogs, and hovering around the crates are throngs of people trying to sit or stand or lean. There must be two hundred people here, cramming themselves into corners and spilling onto every available surface. There's no room for me to set up, forcing me to leave Dusty in a public crate for the day. After taking a few disdainful sniffs, the way an aristocrat might look down his nose at the accommodations at a Motel 6, he drops onto his elbows and sighs.

Now that Dusty's settled, I venture out to find my All Fours colleagues. Miraculously, I spot a few familiar faces on the crowded perimeter of the ring: Cyndi, Andi, Marilyn. I take a moment to appreciate the grouping of these particular women as a kind of triptych of feminine variety. There's Marilyn: raven-haired and imperturbable, she's nearly radioactive with force of will. There's Andi: cool and serene beneath a cloud of wavy blond hair—the kind women go to professional hairdressers to get, though you can tell hers is natural by the way she appears almost annoyed by it, continually pushing aside a flaxen flap from her forehead. (Tell her she's pretty, she'll scoff; tell her her dog is pretty, she'll melt.) And then there's Cyndi: bubbly and brunette, her arms in constant motion as she waves, points, gesticulates, and seems to embrace the entire room; her hair is tightly curled and bounces when she talks, and she talks quite a bit. When she spots me, her eyes light up like I'm the exact person in the universe she most longed to see, though I get the impression she's genuinely that way with everybody.

The chairs are all filled—in fact Cyndi's seated cross-legged on the floor—but I refuse to be shunted to the sidelines again. These are my people now, aren't they? Well, aren't they? I decide to make my way over, if only to say hello. Unfortunately, in this kind of fall-of-Saigon setting even such a simple operation requires a plan of attack and navy SEAL execution. Making my way between the railing and the wall, I spend several minutes climbing over people's feet (and treading on a few of them), before I realize I'm not even halfway to my goal. I consider initiating a mission abort.

But they've all seen me now and are watching me make my way over. I could, I suppose, shrug theatrically to signal defeat and begin dolefully retracing my steps. Both Cyndi and Andi are the kind of girl who'd be sure to understand, or give me the benefit of the doubt if they didn't.

But I'm not so sure about Marilyn. I've allowed our eyes briefly to meet. That steely gaze has already locked onto mine. I've as good as told her "expect me." So I feel obligated to forge ahead.

Marilyn, you see, intimidates me. We've been training together for years, but she's so taciturn I barely know her. Most of the people in our class jabber away like cockatoos, but Marilyn isn't just the quiet type; she's quiet with intent. You can tell she's actively listening, that not a thing is escaping her. And she's listened *to*. When she does condescend to say something—briefly, in as few words as will do the job—all heads swivel to take it in. She also gives the distinct impression of saying just a bit less than she's thinking, which is an extremely rare quality and always intriguing. She is, in short, a natural figure of authority. I've always been a little awkward around those.

What's more, she's a strapping, athletic woman who exudes physicality and power. Even standing in repose, she seems to be daring you to try and knock her down. None of which would be quite so daunting if she weren't also an absolutely phenomenal agility competitor. When she runs her black Lab, River, all that innate power translates into the sheerest grace. They're so clean together, so elegant, they barely stir the air. Watching them is a sobering reminder of how very far I have to go with Dusty.

Suddenly, I wonder what on earth Marilyn, of all people, is doing at a novice trial. I then notice her daughter Eryn, a slight, pretty thing with saucer eyes and an honest-to-God peaches-and-cream complexion, the kind Victorian manuals used to extol. She wouldn't be out of place in a Merchant Ivory film, wearing a bonnet and reading a letter beneath a tree. She's very young—possibly a teenager, though if so a newly-minted one—and I remember her as an actual child, all pink and giggly, from back when I was competing with Carmen. It's a shock to see her suddenly so long of limb, so angular. It's Eryn who's the novice here, and looking into those large, clear eyes I can see another iron-willed competitor in the making. Agility is still a new sport, but it seems to be breeding its first dynasties.

I've arrived just in time to see Cyndi compete in the FAST trial with her boxer, Piper. She qualifies, though complains it's the first time she's ever Q'd without also placing. She jokes about how naked she'll feel going home without a ribbon. From anyone else this might come off as arrogance, but Cyndi is possibly the most jovial human being I've ever met—her good humor is a kind of superpower. As if in infancy she was rocketed to earth from a distant planet where the inhabitants do nothing but laugh.

Andi is up for a title too, in standard, and she has a good chance of winning it. Inexplicably, her golden retriever, Kelly, pops out of the weaves one pole too soon, and Andi doesn't go back to correct the mistake. This costs her a Q. I can see the look of resignation on her face as she moves on, and don't understand it. When she completes her run and comes back to where we're all huddled against the wall, Marilyn is merciless with her: "Why didn't you fix the weaves?"

"I thought I'd already blown it," Andi says, blushing in embarrassment. "We had too many refusals, didn't we?"

"No," Marilyn says, "you didn't. You could've titled, idiot." And with lightning swiftness she reaches out and flicks Andi's forehead.

Almost at once a red welt appears in the middle of Andi's ivory brow. She gasps, then looks at me and says, "She flicked me!"—as if there were something I ought to do about it. She turns back to Marilyn and says, "You're always flicking me! Don't flick me!"

"It's for your own good," says Marilyn, and there's a glint of wicked glee in her eyes. For the first time I realize: Marilyn is funny. Marilyn is a *scamp*. It comes as a bit of a shock. What's more surprising is that these people are so natural around me— even inclusive. I really feel like I've cracked the inner circle now and am seeing what they're like behind the professional facade. Though, admittedly, there remains a little voice in my head admonishing me: "See, you still don't really know them."

The biggest surprise of the day comes during my jumpers run with Dusty. I feel only the most perfunctory degree of performance anxiety, a sizeable chunk of my mind already strategizing the drive home.

The course starts with a tunnel, an unusual opener, but that's good for us—Dusty loves the tunnel. When I'm given the nod from the timer, I send him into it, and when he pops out it's like wham, wham, wham: jump, jump, front cross to the right, jump—then another tunnel, doubling back, jump, jump, jump, jump, reverse cross into a third tunnel, jump again. So far it's been magic—no refusals, no off courses, even decent speed. I can hear myself gasping as I run, but it feels like I'm holding my breath.

We're headed for the penultimate obstacle: the weave poles. There are only six of them in novice, and that's an advantage. Everything depends on nailing the entry: he's got to take the first pole with his left shoulder. He's on my left already, which should make it easier to scoop him right in there. But if he screws it up— I've seen handlers waste an appalling amount of time trying to fix a bad weave-pole entry. Hell, I've *been* one of those handlers. You keep calling the dog back and trying to angle him in again, but he's confused; you've lost your momentum, and you can sense the judge behind you, her hands working madly, signaling refusal after refusal.

Dusty enters the weave poles with his left shoulder. I'm so astonished, I momentarily balk. He balks too, but I recover in time to get him moving again before he can slip out. Second pole, third, fourth—my God, we're going to do it. We're going to nail the weaves on the *first try*.

After the fourth pole he stops to sneeze. I nearly swoon from anxiety. But I will him to continue. What I am saying? I *howl* for him to continue: "*Come on, boy, almost there!*" And then we're through the fifth pole.

And the sixth.

And over the final jump.

For a moment, I'm dizzy, disoriented. There's applause; I can hear people hooting. Then it hits me: we've done it.

We've Q'd.

We have our novice jumpers title.

Glory.

My hands tremble as I take Dusty's leash from the railing and reattach it to him. I feel like I might hyperventilate, so I take him back to the crate, give him some final words of congratulations and a big hug (he stiffens immediately, as if to say, "For God's sake, people are watching"), then make straight for the door and plunge myself into the cold, clear air.

Glory.

Outside there's a parade and fireworks in my head. But the sudden quiet, the chilly mist, and the absence of other people are at odds with my unfettered joy. I try to maintain my euphoria, nurse it along—visualize myself picking up speed toward the national championships—but inevitably the prosaic weight of physical reality crushes all my fantasies of triumph. This really isn't anything to get all excited about. It's just the first step in a long, long process. A novice title, nothing more. Probably dozens of people have picked one up today.

I take a deep breath to put the seal on my new humility, and then head back inside. Just as suddenly as the cold, uncaring outer world had overwhelmed me, once indoors I'm instantly enveloped by *esprit de corps*: greetings, congratulations, joyful smiles from those who improbably, endearingly, treat my success as if it were their own. Andi gives me a big hug and tells me how proud she is; Marilyn tells me she's recorded my run on her video cam, in case I'd like to see it later. I try thanking them, but it comes out sounding so much less than adequate.

"Do you know what you did at the weave poles?" Marilyn asks.

I blink. I have no idea what she's talking about and tell her so.

"You really don't remember?"

I reassure her I don't.

She grins. "When Dusty stopped and sneezed, you actually said gesundheit."

Everyone laughs, and I feel it welling up in me again, despite all my better inclinations toward pragmatism. What the hell—it's just for today:

Glory.

CHAPTER 14

A Day at the Orifice

As it turns out, we didn't merely qualify, we took second place in the sixteen-inch division. A crimson ribbon bearing our names is issued to us, along with a white and gold "new title" ribbon; I place them both on the dashboard as I drive home, thinking perhaps to wow and astonish other drivers on the road.

As we merge onto the highway, I practice saying aloud, "Dusty NAJ." This is the official AKC abbreviation for his new title (Novice Agility Jumpers with Weaves). It trips delightfully off my tongue. I'm confident that it's only the first of a long chain of titles —Dee's Kaleigh, for example, is MACH3 CDX JHV SHFur SHF RE MXF TDI CGC (which looks a lot like what that chimp on the typewriter might produce on his way to *King Lear*)—but for the moment I'm thrilled just to have the one.

When you earn a title on the first day of an agility trial, you can usually request an immediate "move up" so you can compete in your new class on the second day. But this is a novice-only trial, so there's no open class for me to move up to. I could still run in both standard and jumpers tomorrow, but now that we've got our NAJ title only the standard run will count for anything.

This leaves me wondering, on the way home, whether I should even bother coming back. It's an awfully long drive to make for just one run—and as an extra dissuasion the return traffic is beyond heinous. What should be an hour's drive ends up taking three. My fault, for waiting around to the very end of the trial, but I'd wanted to corral the judge into posing for a snapshot with Dusty and me brandishing our ribbons. Well, I have the photo, fine, but now it's costing me. My neck is stiff, my ass cheeks sore, my legs are numb, and my patience has been slowly shredded. I never want to set foot in an automobile again, and to judge by the nervous panting I hear behind me, Dusty feels the same way.

By the time we get home I have a searing headache. I'm supposed to cook dinner tonight—honey-glazed pork tenderloin in a fennel-mascarpone sauce; all the ingredients are sitting primly in the fridge—but I'm too shattered to face the task, so we just order a pizza instead. In the meantime, Jeffrey cracks open a bottle of champagne to celebrate Dusty's first title. Alas, I'm in such a state I can barely enjoy it. Yet I drink three full glasses in a vain attempt to dull the pain.

I lay awake all night, tossing and turning as my head throbs, and I feel like I'm bleeding from my eyes. Somewhere in the ridiculously early hours, I manage to fall asleep from sheer exhaustion, but the alarm clock trills to life soon after. I lie there limp and dazed, feeling worse than I have in a very long time. The crippling headache still has me in its malevolent grip and is enjoying a helping hand from a spanking new hangover. Accent on the "spanking." Well, I'd been waffling over returning to Spring Grove; now

I emphatically decide against it. I'd much prefer just to lie here and wait quietly for death to claim me.

Yet once this decision is made, I feel something inside me—some wriggling, niggling sense of honor—rail against it. "Is this the behavior of a champion?" it says. "One minuscule victory and you retire from the field. That's the great goal you've been chasing? The first difficulty you face, the first physical hardship, and you pack up your single laurel and withdraw? So much for your vaunted ambition."

I roll over, and the inner voice waits for me to readjust on the pillow, then continues: "And what about your friends? They were so supportive of you, so happy for you, and you're not going to be there to return the favor? I guess all that blathering on about community was just a bunch of gushy rhetoric."

The next thing I know I'm on my feet, muttering and groaning as I fight my way into clothes, splash cold water on my face, down a pair of aspirin, and head downstairs, clutching the walls for support. Dusty follows, blinking and yawning—keeping just enough distance to let me know that he's with me only conditionally.

As I pass the living room I smell something sharp, pungent, and unmistakable. I turn on a light and see that, sure enough, sometime during the night Carmen has had a bout of diarrhea in the living room. Whoops—no, two bouts. Hold on—three. In fact it appears she went quite Jackson Pollock in there.

A wave of almost primal despair washes over me, but I fight it back. I've got to man up here. I roll up my sleeves, pick up as much of the mess I can, give the rest a thorough soaking and blotting, and finally run it over with the steam cleaner (which we purchased for just such emergencies). That done, I take Carmen around the block to make sure whatever got into her has now fully worked its way out. She has a few more viscous squats then appears relieved and exhausted. Back in the house, I console her with a brief session of chin scratching, then give her a bowl of bland food with some Cheerios sprinkled on top as a treat. I say a little prayer that I won't see them again later.

It's now too late to have any breakfast myself, but then this unsavory business has killed my appetite. I leash up Dusty and shuttle him out to the car.

When we arrive at the WAG Building, the noise and closeness of the crowd seem even more unendurable than yesterday, possibly due to my sad physical shape. I seek out a public crate for Dusty, but there's only one to be had, and it's very small. I have to insert him like a Thanksgiving turkey into an oven. He gives me a "you've got to be kidding" look. I remind him that it's only temporary.

I run into Carl and Kim, who are hovering around KC and Fletcher's crates. We chat for a while about the cramped conditions, and they tell me they're actually sort of used to it because they live in a condominium. My jaw drops. "You have two Portuguese water dogs, and you live in a condo?"

"Yeah, I know," Carl says with a laugh. "We've got their crates stacked on top of each other to save space, just like they are here, but still . . ."

I'm back up front in time to see Andi qualify in FAST. I congratulate her as she comes off the course, but she tosses it off with a shrug. She's like that: a real team player, always much more emotionally responsive to other people's achievements. Whereas

I'm still motivated principally by dreams of glory. But I can sense myself coming around; I'm genuinely excited by her victory.

We chat for a while on the sidelines, and I mention my astonishment at Carl and Kim's living arrangements. "That's nothing," she says almost dismissively. "I live in a 750-square-foot apartment."

My eyes pop open. "With both Kelly *and* Whisper?" Her two golden retrievers.

She nods then adds, with her habitual dry wit, "It can be interesting."

There's something humbling about this. I live in a three-story house and I still feel like I'm tripping over my dogs—so much so that, I admit it, at times I get frustrated and even irate. "Get out of my goddamn way" is a phrase not infrequently heard under my roof. And yet I've been accustomed to thinking of myself as a dog lover. Well, obviously I am, but, I now realize, of a decidedly lesser stripe. I'd never even dreamed of getting a dog until I had a house and a yard. A very *big* house and yard. These people humble me.

Additional humility is soon on hand in the form of young Eryn, who runs River in FAST. Success, again, greets her easily. The girl is a marvel, really. It's like the laws of physics change when she gets out there. Inanimate objects jump into her path when she requires them and leap away from her when she doesn't. She herself just kind of floats.

So goes the morning. I'm forced to have lunch in my car because there's no room to maneuver my elbows, much less sit down, in the facility. Seated behind the steering wheel, munching away, I try to enjoy the quiet and isolation, which should be balm for my still-clanging headache. Instead I just feel pathetic. For whatever reason, eating alone in your car is pretty much a benchmark of Scandinavian despair. With the rain spattering against the windshield, I feel like a character in a Bergman film, except I'm almost certainly eating better food: a roast-beef sandwich with Gorgonzola and red onion. You'd never find Liv Ullmann partaking of anything quite so robust—or eating at all, now that I think of it. I suppose I could've brought Dusty out for company, but it's coming down just steadily enough to make that a bad idea. I don't want him even remotely slippery when he runs.

Wet feet, it turns out, might have been preferable to the conditions in which I left him. When I return to the crate, I find the Skye terrier lodged above him going determinedly berserk. As I get nearer, a stout woman—presumably its owner—goes up to the cage and shrieks, "*Shuuuut uuup!*" I wonder, with sudden alarm, how frequently she's been doing *that*.

I panic for a second because it looks as though someone has removed Dusty from the crate, but no, there he is, in the very back, pressed against one corner with a look on his face of such inconsolable misery that my guilt nearly knocks me back a full step. I unlatch the door and take him out—he's as limp as a rag doll—and coo in his ear, stroke him, tell him I'm sorry, I didn't realize I'd left him in a pressure-cooker, that everything's going to be all right. "We'll just do our run, boy—just one run, and then we can go home. You don't even have to Q. Just get through it and we'll go."

By now my lunch is sitting uneasily in my stomach, and I feel a kind of brisk gastric cha-cha get under way. It probably would've been better if sometime during the past dozen-odd hours I'd voided my gut of all the bile and toxins that have accumulated there, but the simple fact is that I haven't thrown up since 1979.

Many people refuse to believe me when I tell them this—as though I've claimed to be able to fly or to have met Shakespeare—but it doesn't seem so extraordinary to me. Vomiting is, after all, an extreme reaction to extreme conditions, and by dint of discipline, moderation, and a bit of luck, I've skirted those extremities. No drunk has been dead enough, no flu severe enough, to provoke me to toss my cookies, and for the most part I have no problem with that. From what I remember of puking, it's not a felicitous activity. But at times like these I can see it has its uses, and as I stand in the hole with Dusty, hearing Krakatoan rumblings from my deep interior, it seems vastly preferable to have endured the indignity of being sick on a roadside shrubbery than to face a sixteen-obstacle gauntlet at a jogging clip.

The dog ahead of us—a cocker spaniel named Shiner—is midway into her run, and we're getting ready to go on the line, when the by-now familiar sound of Dusty's regurgitative warm-up reaches my ear. I look down just in time to see him spew up a big glob of sulfur-colored foam. "That's it," I tell myself. "It's empirically proven: I am absolutely projecting my own infirmities onto my dog. And pretty goddamn specifically too."

I feel a surge of panic; Shiner is heading for the finish. We should be on line, ready to go. Instead I'm standing here with a woozy Sheltie and a pool of sick. What the hell do I do? Fortunately, Andi, supportive soul that she is, has chosen this moment to come by and wish me good luck. She's seen what's happened, waves me on, and shouts, "Don't worry about it. I'll take are of it—just go!"

Despite Andi's charity, my nerves are all ajangle as we head out to the line. I put Dusty in a sit-stay and head to the first obstacle, a simple jump, then turn back to face him. I can't help looking past him to where Andi is on her hands and knees, mopping up the flooring with paper towels. I always knew she was an unflaggingly positive person, but this sort of support I could never have expected from a fellow hobbyist. I'm starting to recognize that this group is there for each other through thick and thin (and apparently foamy). How do you even begin to thank someone for that? Flowers? Possibly. In any color but yellow.

I snap to attention and call for Dusty to come. The first jump goes easily enough, but it's straight downhill from there. I'm still ill and anxious, and as a result he is too. He bails off the A-frame, refuses the teeter, and his weave-pole entry is about as accurate as if I'd dropped him onto it from a plane. We hobble off the course, barely ambulatory.

I take just enough time to thank Andi profusely for help above and beyond, and to wish everyone good luck on their jumpers runs, because as much as I'd like to stay and be supportive, I'm in desperate shape and so is my dog.

Back on the road, with the window lowered just enough to allow some invigorating autumn air to bathe my face, I begin to feel somewhat restored. It's a few hours earlier than we departed yesterday so the roads aren't nearly as bad. My head, slowly and by degrees, begins to clear.

Still, it's been a pretty rough day right from the get-go, and I have to wonder if there's an element of hubris at play here. After all, I was more than a tad cocky yesterday, swanning around with my new title and my pair of ribbons, dreaming about glory and getting all chummy with the judge. The gods have accordingly spent this ensuing day slapping me back down to my proper place in the dirt. Maybe that's the way it'll always be, any success inevitably triggering a cosmic backlash.

"Never mind, it's over," I say, looking at Dusty in the rearview mirror. "We got through it, and we're still in one piece. Right, boy?" He shoots me a ghastly, panicked grimace; he's panting more than usual. "For God's sake, I wish you'd just *relax*." But not much has changed since that first drive we took together. He hasn't learned to sit or recline in the car, insisting instead on standing bolt upright, acting like it's his job to ward off imminent disaster.

Still, he seems a little more distraught than usual today. I don't think anything about it till forty minutes into the drive, when I'm suddenly accosted by a wave of fecal funk. "Oh God no," I say aloud, and I swerve quickly over to the side of the road. I jump out of the car, throw open the back door, and discover that, just as I feared, Dusty has unleashed a torrent of diarrhea on the backseat. The gods clearly aren't through with me yet. And with classical symmetry, they've decided to bookend my day with quantities of liquid shit.

"It's all right, boy," I tell him, unhooking him from his seat harness and taking him to the side of the road. He sits with his head hung in shame, making himself very small, almost embryonic. "It's not your fault," I add consolingly. But I can't help thinking that it *is* his fault. I always give him plenty of time to graze the grass before we start on any long drive. I can't be blamed if he's wound himself up too tightly take advantage of it.

Or can I? Didn't I just this afternoon determine conclusively that my early suspicions were dead on? That I'm the big bad behind all his aberrations?

Fortunately, I still have one more old towel on hand and a large bottle of mineral water in the trunk. A skillful application of both soon has the backseat looking (if not quite smelling) as good as new. I make a scientific note that diarrhea is much more absorbent than vomit; a fact that future generations (or my car's next owner) will surely wish to know.

I leave the soiled towels by the side of the road. I know it's littering, but I'm too stressed out to think of any other means of disposing of them. As atonement to the planet, I make a deal with myself to write a check to Greenpeace or the Sierra Club when I get home.

"Okay," I say, as I snap Dusty back into place and head around to the driver's door, "I have officially had enough of bodily discharges today."

Once it's passed my lips, I wish I hadn't said it. This isn't a day to be tempting fate.

A few hours (and much soap and scalding water) later, I finally cook my pork tenderloin. But something seems slightly off. I keep wrinkling my nose suspiciously, checking the bottom of my shoes, having a quick look into the next room. There's nothing, but the habit persists. I realize my sensory lobes may have been ever so slightly traumatized today.

The behavior continues into dinner, so that finally Jeff asks, "Why are you sniffing like that? What do you smell?"

"Never mind," I say. "It's really best if you don't know."

And I'll tell you what: I'm not much liking the look of that mascarpone sauce either.

CHAPTER 15

Magic Time

One last outdoor trial to cap the season. Another chance at coupling our jumpers title with a standard title. A mere baby step toward becoming a champ but a maddeningly elusive one. I'm sitting in the shade of Betsy's "easy up"—a kind of tent without tent flaps—and the air is mild and crisp.

As we sit gabbing, a small, wiry woman walks by, wearing a tracksuit seemingly made from the same material as FedEx envelopes. She's leading her bull terrier to the standard ring and is trilling to him in a voice that makes Minnie Mouse sound like Bea Arthur: "Come on, sweetie, it's *showtime*! It's *showtime*!"

I can't suppress a chuckle, and when the woman is out of earshot, I jerk my thumb in her direction. "There's some serious motivation goin' on there."

Dee gives me a sly look and says, "You don't know the half of it."

"Hmm?" I say. "Don't know the half of what?"

"Her motivational techniques," says Dee with an impish grin.

"So, wait, you've really never heard this before? You don't know about Joellen?"

I sometimes forget that Dee knows virtually everyone on the agility circuit. And by "knows" them, I mean has them pegged, categorized, and nailed down tight. And by the way she's said the name Joellen, I can tell there is infamy in it.

"No, I don't know her," I say, shifting expectantly in my seat. "Is that a trademark of hers? The 'showtime' thing?"

"Yes," Dee replies, and she leans in a little, a conspiratorial move that thrills me utterly. "But what's way more interesting is that before 'showtime,' there's 'magic time.'"

"'Magic time,'" I repeat slowly, with emphasis.

She nods. "Mm-hmm."

I wait for more, but clearly she's going to make me earn my gratification by supplying the correct prompts. And I'm just stubborn enough not to want to. So I hold off a moment, wondering if her eagerness to tell me will overtake her desire for me to beg.

And then someone new pops her head in to say hello—someone from outside the All Fours "family"—and the moment is lost. Dee's attention turns to the newcomer, who trails a pair of nervous Havanese whose thrusting about sets off all the other dogs in their crates. I end up removing Dusty from the confusion, and the "magic time" thread is irretrievably lost.

I don't even recall it myself until later in the day, when I'm on my way to the Porta-Johns. To my dismay, I find three people in line waiting for one of the two units to become available. That's not really a lot of people—unless you're really singin' the "Burstin' Bladder Blues." Which, at this moment, I am. I honestly *cannot* wait. And given my extreme aversion to the condition of the average Porta-John several hours into its daylong lifespan, I decide to avail myself of nature's bountiful flora to accomplish my task.

There's a ring of shrubbery not far off, around a small, still pond—it's the only cover around, and rather obvious, so the risk of discovery isn't small. But I only need about ninety seconds, so I figure what the hell.

I'm just enjoying the floaty feeling that comes with having lessened the pressure on the kidneys by a factor of ten when I hear something not far: a familiar, piping kind of singsong: "Come on, honey! It's magic time!"

I move aside a branch and peer through the intervening foliage. I see Joellen, and her bull terrier, and I realize I've stumbled onto the elusive secret of magic time.

And what I see—well.

Well.

Joellen is doing something to her dog.

Something that he, lacking an opposable thumb, can't do for himself.

He seems to enjoy it, wiggling his legs and huffing. And the way she's working her wrist, I can tell she's done this many times before.

For a few brutal moments I'm absolutely mesmerized, but I certainly don't want to stick around to witness the happy ending. I bustle from the bushes and skipper back to the tent rather determinedly.

By some fluke of fate, I find Dee alone. She looks at me a bit perplexedly—possibly my face registers some kind of unease—and I blurt, "Is that even *legal*?"

"What?" she asks.

I screw up my face. "Magic time!"

"Oh," she says, with a wry smile. "Someone told you?"

"No no. I just stumbled across the free demo."

Dee whistles. "Well, that puts you a leg up on the rest of us."

"Don't say 'leg up,'" I beg her, and I lower myself back into my chair. Still flailing for some way to express my horror and astonishment, I say, "Why does she do this thing?"

Dee shrugs. "She says it calms him down."

"Calms him . . ." Again words fail me. I feel like I need a new language, something beyond English or any other terrestrial tongue, to express what I'm feeling. Like something from *On Beyond Zebra!* "Next we have *kwiff* / You can look it right up / Kwiff stands for *kwiffenzip* / That's palmin' your pup."

"But," I continue, "wouldn't you *want* your dogs to be a little pumped up, a little eager, when you're running the course? Seems to me calmness would be a *dis*advantage."

"She says it helps him focus. Takes away any interest he might have in following scents on the course or being distracted by what's going on in the other ring."

I start to speak, but first glance over my shoulder to make sure Joellen isn't within earshot. "It's okay," Dee tells me. "You don't have to worry about her hearing you. Heck, she'll tell you all about it herself. How'd you think I found out?"

"You're kidding. She openly admits it?"

"*Brags* about it." Dee can't help laughing at how unsettled I am.

I decide to take Dusty for a walk and try to regain my sense of, well, reality. As I zip him out of his crate, I can't help recalling the several occasions I've caught him wiggling around on his back, enjoying a good, solid erection. The sight of that quivering appendage—it looks like a lipstick twisted all the way out of its tube—is alarming enough; the idea of actually grabbing hold of it and gettin' down to business is just flat-out unimaginable. I can't think of anything more perverse.

But am I being too fainthearted? I'm accustomed to thinking of my dogs as companions: entities analogous, if not equal, to myself. Any sort of sexual contact with them would therefore seem to be an expression of that relationship. But would it have to be? I've often noted that people who work with animals tend to regard them more as biological constructs than reflections of their own identities. Even certain agility people are like this. At my very first trial, on a sweltering summer day in July, a woman I was chatting with (about the heat, of course) excused herself to go apply some ice to her dog's testicles. I found this startling on two counts: First, the idea of groping around Grifter's gonads just isn't something to be tossed off casually in conversation. Second, if anyone ever slapped an ice pack to my own sack of sixpence I'd likely launch right into the next county.

And yet, the more I thought about it the more sense it made. The skin of the scrotum is very thin, so the fastest way to cool the entire bloodstream would be to do so from that locality. A dog owner should approach these things practically, shouldn't he? Animals have no sense of squeamishness over body parts or bodily functions, no concept of privacy or modesty. They can't be offended. Surely Joellen's solution to her dog's agility problem is predicated on nothing more than rational expediency. There's nothing prurient or salacious in it; it's—therapeutic. Or so I tell myself.

I'm just leading Dusty past the ring when I notice that Joellen is now running, and I'm compelled to stop and watch. Almost immediately I sense trouble; her dog is loping along, obviously enjoying himself tremendously, and certainly he's not fixed on any distractions within the ring or without. But just as noticeably he's not fixed on Joellen—at least, not to the degree he should be. He's missing any sense of urgency, of mission, which, given what he's apparently just been through, isn't hard to imagine. If I were in a similar situation—asked to slip on some Nikes and jump a bunch of hurdles right after someone's gone and flown me to the moon—I'm guessing I wouldn't set any land speed records.

In fact the dog is sloppy, eventually cutting it too close and dropping a bar, instantly NQ'ing. Not that he cares; he keeps sailing along, smiling widely, his tongue lolling lazily in the breeze. He's the picture of amused contentment, not competitive zeal. Joellen, to her credit, runs him through the rest of the course anyway—actual ring experience is rare enough that you shouldn't bail on it even after you're out of the running. In that respect, she's not a complete lunatic.

All the same, what the hell is she thinking? I find myself wondering this again as she hooks up her dog at the finish gate and turns our way. She's heading directly for us; in fact she's going to pass right by me. I realize I can find out what's going on in her mind just by *asking* her. Dee says she's only too happy to discuss "magic time." Accordingly, I start rehearsing my opening gambit: "Excuse me, ma'am, my name is Rob. I wonder if I might ask you about your unusual method of preperformance stress relief . . ."

I clear my throat as she comes parallel to me; she even looks me in the eye and smiles. But I can't bring myself to speak. A moment later, she's moved on and the opportunity has vanished. And really, it's just as well I didn't introduce myself.

Not entirely keen to shake her hand.

CHAPTER 16

Alley Oops

As a dog walker of some years' experience, I've acquired a kind of sixth sense—an ability to predict potential trouble before it's otherwise perceptible. It's an especially vital attribute when you're walking more than one animal at the same time. I'm almost prescient in my awareness of threats that lurk around corners, whether they take the form of bicycles (why, oh why, do people persist in riding them on sidewalks?), large gangs of stampeding kids, or (most perilous of all) stray dogs.

As a result, I've been able to steer clear of some highly dicey situations, something my dogs don't always appreciate (Dusty in particular—he always prefers to confront danger head-on). But the law of averages is against you in the long run. If you walk your dogs every day, three times a day, in a city neighborhood teeming with hazards, eventually you'll run smack into something nasty. And odds are you won't be ready for it.

Take today. Our walk starts out as usual, with Dusty pulling ahead of me, Carmen lagging behind. This can make them a bit difficult to maneuver, especially since, as herding dogs, they periodically circle around me before resuming their preferred positions. It's a juggling act, but I've gotten pretty good at it. Though from afar, I'm sure I look like a Radio City chorus girl. A better solution would be to take them separately, but that would double my walk time from one hour to two.

Suddenly, I spot another dog walker coming at us from the opposite direction. This isn't always a red flag; Carmen loves meeting new friends, and I can easily restrain Dusty while she makes her introductions. But there's a premonitory tickle at the base of my skull: something about the approaching dog—big, brown, rangy—is warning me off a close encounter.

No big deal. This kind of thing happens all the time. And the good thing about city neighborhoods is that there's always somewhere else to go: across the street, around the corner, or, in this case, up an alley. I don't usually go in for alleys—the dogs find the spilled garbage much more fascinating than I'd like—but they'll do in a pinch. And this is a pinch.

It's a residential block, so most of the buildings here are single-family homes or six-flat apartment buildings whose garages and backyards abut the alley. We pass battered iron doors, gang graffiti, wan-looking clutches of weeds. We're about a third of the way through when a gate suddenly swings open and a slack-looking woman in flip-flops appears holding a plastic garbage bag. She looks at me, I look at her, and before either of us can even register the glance something darts out from behind her legs—a streak of black and tan—and suddenly it's all over Dusty.

The woman screams—and I mean *screams*; compared to this

gal, Fay Wray was mealymouthed—and I realize, a beat later, that we're being attacked by an enormous rottweiler.

I remain calm and give the woman the benefit of the doubt. After all, there have been a few occasions when one of my own dogs has gotten away from me and gone lunging after some presumed rival. I know the feeling. I understand. I sympathize. More importantly, I know how to get my dog back under control within seconds. This woman, however, is utterly hopeless. She's down on all fours, scrambling after her rottie, still screaming as though she were being thrown into a wood chipper. Finally, she grabs him and I'm able to pull Dusty back to me, but then the rottie wriggles away from her and attacks Carmen, who lets out such a pitiful yelp that my calm demeanor snaps. Violating every rule of how to conduct yourself in a dogfight, I stick my hand into the fray and try to grab the rottie's collar. He neatly evades me, leaving just enough opening for a frantic Carmen to bite me good and hard.

I withdraw my wounded hand and turn to the woman, who's still clambering around on her hands and knees and screaming bloody murder. *"Get hold of your dog!"* I command her.

"I caaaaan't!" she howls, and she grabs wildly at him, managing to hold him a few scant seconds before he jerks free and goes after Dusty again.

This time Dusty is ready; in fact he's spoilin' for it. I try to reel him back in, but he's so worked up that he chomps into my thigh. So far, I'm the only one taking any hits here. But this can't go on; my dogs are Shelties, for God's sake—lump them together, they don't weigh as much as this rottie's head.

And that's when I realize I'm living every dog walker's nightmare. I'm faced with a threat I didn't see coming and can't control. Everything's a blur of fur and saliva, and I can't think straight because of the snarling and yelping and screaming. Every few seconds the woman gets a grip on her dog, and I think, "It's over," then he pulls away from her again and goes after one of mine. Dusty is making noises I've never heard before; his eyes are wild; his fur is matted. Meanwhile Carmen's on her side, her hind legs knotted up in her leash—she's helpless and mewling.

Finally, after the next wave of the attack, I haul off and kick the rottie in the flank, which sends him skittering across the alley. All hundred-ass pounds of him. It feels like I've broken every bone in my foot.

Now, it takes a hell of a lot of provocation for me to kick a dog, and I immediately feel bad about it. After all, he's clearly not the one responsible. It's his idiot owner, who hasn't trained him and can't control him, who's at fault here (a well-placed kick in *her* flank would be entirely more appropriate, and over the next several days I'll console myself by playing this very image over and over in my head). But at this point it was do or die—perhaps literally.

While the rottie is recovering, I rein in my Shelties and run like sixty. Just get the high holy hell outta Dodge.

I don't know how long this whole fracas has gone on, but apparently long enough to attract onlookers. I suppose the woman's bloodcurdling shrieks were enough to guarantee that. As I spill out of the mouth of the alley, a few people ask, "Are you okay?" But I don't pause to reply—I don't want to stop till I'm at least a block away. The rottie might be hoofing it after me for all I know.

I'm sure as hell not going to lose a half-second peering over my shoulder to make sure.

When we're far enough away to feel safe, I slow down and rein in my dogs. They're both agitated, but they look all right. I run my hands over them, taking stock—everything seems to be in place. A couple of patches of missing fur, but no wounds. I can scarcely believe the luck.

We haven't had our full hour's walk, but I'm too badly shaken to resume it. I'd be jumping out of my skin at the sound of twigs snapping. Also, I have a few wounds of my own to see to—one from each of my dogs. But I have to give them a pass: they bit out of confusion and fear.

As we head back, I notice that neither Dusty nor Carmen seems particularly fazed by what they've been through. In fact Dusty is walking with a little macho strut, as though he's gone four rounds with the world featherweight champ and left the ring intact. I'm reminded, again, that dogs are dogs—conflict and combat are just how they do business. What he doesn't have a grasp on is that street brawling can be lethal, especially if your opponent's mass is about fifteen times your own. I can scarcely expect Dusty to know that I've actually just saved his life. No doubt he's pretty well convinced he could have handled things on his own. He really, honestly has no idea how small he is. If he did, he wouldn't be so keen to take on U-Haul trailers.

Eventually, my adrenaline wears off, and I realize that while my dogs may be fine I'm hurt far worse than I imagined. I'm still limping, and sometime during the melee I seem to have massively wrenched by back. It's agonizing to sit down, no less painful to stand, and there's no relief in lying down. I'm a real mess. Jeffrey's away on another business trip, so I've got to be my own nursemaid. I bandage my wounds and tape up my foot, then pop a few painkillers and call it an early night.

As I lie in bed, trying to wind down with a bit of light reading (Cicero's scathingly bitchy "Second Philippic Against Antony"—I never get tired of it), Dusty leaps up on the bed and puts his face close to mine. It's his nightly routine. As always, I say "kiss," and he very lightly swipes his tongue across the tip of my nose. Sometimes, if he's feeling particularly affectionate, he'll allow me to massage his forelegs while he stands bolt upright, looming over me, but tonight he's not in the mood. Satisfied that I'm down for the duration, he hops off and trundles across the hall to my office, where, as always, he curls up on the couch for the night.

I'm wracked with pain, bandaged and bruised, and dopey from self-medication. Whereas he, weighing not quite twenty pounds soaking wet, is perfectly fine after going mano a mano with a rottweiler the size of a Ford Escort.

"This is precisely the worst danger of being in a dogfight," my friend Haven says when I e-mail her about the incident the next day. "Collateral damage. I think it's akin to being shot with one's own gun." But she's not at all sanguine about it—in fact her message starts with, "You were attacked by a rottweiler? If I were actually the fainting type, I would swoon."

"I didn't have time to swoon," I write back. "It all happened so quickly. Or, rather, it seemed to be happening in slow motion; my mind was working furiously, but I couldn't get my body to keep up. It was more infuriating than anything else. It wasn't till I got home and tried to unhook the dogs and couldn't get my fingers to work that I thought, 'Hmm, perhaps I've had just a hint of trauma.' The dogs, however, were completely untroubled."

"Of course they were," she replies. "They were being dogs. You, however, were being a person who got tangled up in dogs. But the swoony part for me is you referring to the 'sixth wave' of the attack."

"Six at *least*," I clarify. "Fortunately, at the time I was too angry to be terrified."

"I can't believe no one died. I'm sorry to say it like this, but the rottweiler must not have intended to kill your dogs. Am I wrong?"

I have to think about this awhile. Haven has the most unerring dog sense of anyone I know. She's also almost supernaturally in synch with what the general public considers the more violent breeds—pit bulls, Dobermans, rottweilers. She loves and understands them. If this is her read on the situation, I have to take it seriously.

And of course it takes only a moment's reflection to realize she's right. For God's sake, Dusty and Carmen are Shelties. Bouncy little herding dogs about the size and heft of your average stuffed animal. Whereas the rottie is a full-bore killing machine. There was no way I, or his owner, or any power short of military ordnance could have prevented him from tearing my dogs to bits and flossing his teeth with their gut strings, if that's what he'd wanted.

"I was *amazed* there were no wounds," I write back. "So yes, I think you're right; he didn't set out to kill. Or even maim. Just to exert his territorial rights. But of course I didn't know that at the time."

"Rottweilers are very tricky," Haven agrees. "The best dog I ever had, Roxanne, was a rottie, and she truly didn't have an aggressive bone in her body—not to other dogs, not to people. But she also didn't posture; she didn't bark, didn't make a show of anything. Then I realized: oh, she will simply kill someone, should I be threatened someday."

After this exchange, I spend a humbling afternoon reflecting on the incident. I've been so puffed up and proud of what I call my "dog smarts," yet in the heat of a real emergency I acted like a neophyte. Dropped my guard, put myself in unnecessary jeopardy, and—worst of all—*kicked a dog.*

I've given over a sizable chunk of my life to adopting, training, and competing alongside canines. And yet in many ways I've still got so much to learn. Possibly, I've allowed the comforting structure of the agility world to define my entire relationship with dogs, forgetting that that structure is artificial, imposed on the animals by us. But isn't that why I started on agility training back in my days with Carmen? Because I felt that my dogs would *enjoy* the structure, even thrive on mastering it?

Yet outside such egalitarian confines, each breed is different: each has its own specific proclivities and characteristic behaviors, and even within a breed those traits alter radically from dog to dog.

It's almost enough to make me regret not having chosen cats.

(I said "almost.")

CHAPTER 17

Hounds for the Holidays

Winter arrives. In Chicago this can mean appalling quantities of snow or frigid, heart-stopping cold. In a good winter, we'll have a few memorable instances of each, just to keep us from forgetting that we are in fact nature's bitch. In a bad winter, we'll be pounded with one right after the other, alternating blows that leave us reeling. And every once in a while we'll have a terrible winter, in which we actually get both calamities at the same time. This is shaping up to be a terrible winter.

It's eleven below zero and snowing briskly when Dusty and I set out for Milwaukee and our first overnight agility trial. In fact we'll be staying two nights so that we can compete in three consecutive days of the Cream City Canines Agility Club trial. I'm hoping a three-day trial will break the run of bad luck we've had with two-day trials, which have been a series of depressingly similar, lackluster performances. Possibly, the extra day will be just what Dusty needs to grow accustomed to the venue and the people and build a modicum of confidence and, who knows, even honest-to-God ambition.

This Cream Cities trial is more popularly known as Hounds for the Holidays (or just Hounds, for short). It's a highlight on the All Fours calendar, and this year is no exception. Almost a dozen of us will be there. I'm especially looking forward to it since it's my first time—I never attended with Carmen.

And now I remember why. The snowfall has reduced visibility to almost nil, and with the sun not yet risen, my headlights are reflecting off the whirling flakes as they spiral toward my windshield. The effect is potentially mesmerizing—and thus potentially lethal. I have to keep adjusting my vision, trying to see beyond the storm; it requires some serious concentration. In the meantime, I can't seem to stop trembling; the temperature climbs a bit (to a balmy six below), and the heater's on full, but my body won't adjust. This is where a good breakfast would've come in handy. I'm usually Breakfast Boy, but this morning I woke up late and had to hurry out of the house to beat the Thursday morning traffic. My first walk-through is scheduled for 8:10, and it's at least a ninety minute drive to Milwaukee. So my stomach's growling and my limbs are shaking as we speed through the dark in a vortex of shimmering snow.

Where the heater has failed me, the music steps in to dispel the chill. I've rather cannily chosen a disc of music by the Argentine composer Astor Piazzolla, whose torrid, tango-driven sound world soon envelopes me and makes me feel, well, not quite like I'm on a beach, but at least like I'm wearing a Panama hat.

We arrive at Uihlein Soccer Park well before eight, leaving sufficient time to unfold Dusty's crate and set up shop. The facility is enormous, the largest I've seen yet. There are three courts, one of which is dedicated solely to excellent standard, another to excellent jumpers. The remaining ring is for all novice and open classes. Crating areas have been marked off by tape around the perimeter, and there's additional space on the mezzanine level, which also hosts a variety of vendors including a masseur (for both handlers *and* dogs) and the inevitable concession stand selling nothing I'd ever eat.

The All Fours setup is pretty easy to spot, since some of the gang arrived late last night and claimed one of the more desirable bits of real estate, where the corridors leading to the front and side doors intersect. There's to be a prize for the best decoration of a crating space and Dee is taking this very seriously; when I arrive, she and some of the others are busy stringing twinkly lights over an expansive yuletide display that includes a "Naughty List" and a "Nice List" on which passersby are welcome to scrawl their nominations. Busy as she is, she manages a brilliant smile and a big hello. She seems utterly in her element, the chaos and confusion seeming to add ballast to her, making her physically more present, in the same way they tend, paradoxically, to render me more diffuse and unmoored. Possibly it's because I'm a writer, but the sight of all these faces—and the particular narrative that shines out of each one of them— is completely distracting to me. I could dissolve in a fit of empathy. Whereas Dee, I think, sees in each face another building block of the world she's spent so many years constructing. She's at home; I'm at sea.

And as usual, my uncertainty translates directly into Dusty's. He slinks along behind me, fretful and wide eyed, trying to look in each direction at once, sensing menace in all of them. Whenever we stop, he leans into me, lifting his front paw as though ready in an instant to leap into my arms or perhaps propel himself through the roof.

For his sake I try to focus and gather my resources. I don't lack self-confidence, but it needs to be summoned. And it helps to see so many familiar faces here: Marilyn, Gus, Deb, Sue, Diane, Alise, Betsy, Cyndi—some I know less well than others, but from what I've heard, Hounds is where the All Fours crew really lets its hair down.

But first there's the actual competition. Now that Dusty and I have our novice jumpers title, we've moved up to the big leagues: open jumpers. It's trickier than novice—more obstacles, tighter turns, twelve weave poles instead of six, and a shorter time to manage it all—but I'm hoping for a breakthrough this weekend. Accordingly, I take all the time allotted to the walk-through.

Still, it seems unreasonable to ask Dusty to Q on the very first day of competition. "Although," I tell him as we await our turn to run, "it's our last trial of the year, and it'd be sweet to go out on a high note. But," I add hastily, as he darts me a look more than usually penetrating, "no pressure."

I needn't have worried. So far from feeling pressure, he performs the run as though nothing at all were required of him. We might be on a picnic for all the urgency he displays, and this despite my increasingly shrill prompting. "Dus-*teeeee,*" I howl as he veers inexorably away from me, like a planet in elliptical orbit. At one point my shrillness actually hurts my own ears.

After it's over, I linger a while to watch the next several runs, just to reassure myself that I'm not the only competitor to bollix his chances. But this salve to my ego quickly evaporates when I go back an hour later to check the score sheet. Dusty and I have clocked in at sixty-seven seconds. No one else even comes close to being so spectacularly overtime. Even the dog who crapped on the table at least managed to be quicker about it.

Disheartened, I collapse Dusty's crate, lead him out to the car, and drive to our hotel. Seeing him in the vast, oppressively clean lobby is a little startling. He seems smaller and bristlier than ever, like I'm dragging a vegetable brush at the end of my leash.

We get to our room—large, pale, antiseptic—and I unhook him while I reopen his crate. He sniffs around the walls and furnishings. "No marking," I warn him, so he gives up and just watches me work. I set out bowls of food and water—he disdains both.

"Look," I tell him, "I'm famished, so I'm going to leave you here for a while to chill. I'll come get you in time for your standard run. Okay?"

He gives me a look that says "very much not okay," then comes up and places a paw on my thigh. This is about as cuddlesome as he ever gets. In fact in his personal repertoire of gestures, it borders on molestation. I can't just ignore such a potent appeal for my physical presence; not with those lemurlike eyes boring into mine so pathetically. "All right, all right," I say, and I order up a sandwich from room service, then settle onto the bed for an hour or so, taking up the novel I've been reading (Dawn Powell's delightfully acid *The Happy Island*). Dusty curls up at my feet and snoozes.

He seems fully rested, if still a bit disoriented, by the time I pile him back in the car for the return drive to Uihlein Soccer Park. I quickly discover that there's been some drama while I've been away; Dee, while seated cross-legged on the floor and watching the excellent jumpers with Kaleigh, was attacked by an Australian shepherd, which had apparently been giving her the woolly eye for several minutes beforehand. Dee was alert enough to forestall any harm, shielding Kaleigh and turning her back on the Aussie before it reached her. I blush, thinking back on my experience with the rottweiler. It's not as if any of the All Fours crew would pass judgment on my for kicking that marauding beast, but it humbles me to think how much I have to learn about handling animals the way Dee does.

That said, the incident has upset her, particularly because the Aussie's negligent owner didn't even bother to apologize. She is now in a white rage. I've never seen her like this. She seems to be giving off static electricity. I'm afraid to get too close to her lest my digital watch go haywire.

I turn to Dusty and whisper, "See what you made me miss?"

As Dusty and I head off for our standard walk-through, I hear angry twitters from the All Fours tent—they plan on taking the attack, and the Aussie owner's poor behavior, to "the committee." I push aside sudden Big Brother fantasies of a cabal of iron-fisted autocrats who rule the agility circuit like Satlin's politburo (might we show up tomorrow and find all trace of the Aussie's owner's identity erased from existence?) and turn my attention to the course.

It looks tricky: sixteen obstacles arranged in a swooping, rabbit-ear configuration—but at least the teeter doesn't crop up till halfway into the run. If I can build up some momentum, maybe Dusty will actually just go ahead and barrel right over it.

No such luck. He follows refusal with refusal, to the point that I have to wonder what he thinks we're doing out here anyway, just having a nice stroll among all this pretty equipment? After he turns his nose up at the teeter, I decide to hell with the course, let's just go for speed—see how soon I can get him over the finish line.

Not very fast, as it happens. Even ignoring the last few obstacles and making a beeline for the gate, he never picks up his pace. It's one of my ongoing frustrations with him; he's a very, very fast dog—I know this from having watched him tear across our backyard, spraying clots of earth behind him—but he never shows it in the ring. He's yet to make the switch from trot to gallop, and I'm determined to get him there. All our friends and supporters are here, rooting for us and lending us their energy and spark. This is our weekend. I have to believe it.

The intensity at the All Fours area has ebbed a bit when we return, but the Aussie attack remains the chief subject of discussion. I don't have much to add, because I didn't see the event, and frankly the whole idea of a committee unnerves me a bit, and I prefer to remain well under its radar. As I pack up and say good night, the others insist I join them for dinner in a few hours. From feeling a bit extraneous—having after all missed the attack, which appears to be today's unifying event—I'm taken aback that I've been asked to come along. But I'm grateful to be included (even though they're only going to Applebee's) and immediately accept. Funny, despite all the hours I've now put in with these people, I still feel a little awkward and self-conscious around them. And while I may consider them friends, I'm happy to have this new evidence that they feel the same.

Dinner is a convivial affair. I order beef, which is usually a safe bet in such places—there's only so much harm you can inflict on a steak, and even then there are bottled sauces to mask the damage. In addition I have three (or is it four?) glasses of zinfandel, and the warmth of the wine magically melts away all the day's insecurities. At one point I seem to be aware of talking too much, yet can't seem to stop.

During my ride back to the hotel with Gus and Deb, my tongue has been loosened to the point at which I might say anything, but Deb, God bless her, never gives me the chance. Her ongoing narrative also serves the valuable function of counteracting the zinfandel and keeping me awake till we pull up to the front entrance of the hotel where, despite the frigid cold, several other guests are out walking their dogs. The arctic air hits me like a slap in the face; I'd like nothing better than to curl up under some nice warm blanket till morning, but such is the joy of being a dog owner—Dusty needs a pee break.

As we head down in the elevator, I become aware that he's looking at me oddly; I realize I'm talking aloud to him, something I almost never do. At least not about baggage-claim turnstiles, which seems to be the subject I've landed on, God only knows why.

I zip up tightly, attempting to lock out the latest onslaught of eyeball-freezing air, and take Dusty around to the back of the building, figuring he'll be likelier to do his business with fewer strangers looking on. And indeed it's suitably isolated here; also quite dark. Then something happens very fast and there's somebody lying on the sidewalk, moaning. A moment later I realize it's me. I've slipped on the ice and knocked the wind right out of myself. I lie there for few seconds in dazed disbelief, then locate my glasses, which are resting in the snow about a yard to my left. As soon as I don them, I can see Dusty staring down at me with growing concern. I try to rise, but I've badly twisted my ankle.

"Help me up," I order him, and as soon as I say it I realize how ridiculous it is. He has all the heft of a stick insect. The only thing he can raise is my expectations.

I consider unhooking him so he at least can return to safety while I lie here and let a frigid death claim me. But then I realize, antisocial as he is, he'd only run farther away from the hotel and thus perish too, so it's up to me to save us both. With a heroic (and rather noisy) effort I get to my feet, or rather to my foot, since I can't put any weight on the injured one without hideous agony.

As I grimace in pain, it occurs to me that this is the same foot with which I kicked the savage rottweiler several weeks ago. There's poetic justice for you. I wish I had a rottweiler now; I could ride it back to the lobby. Instead I'm reduced to hopping, which is such a good idea when you're drunk and on a field of ice and you've already fallen once. Just a really excellent idea. I could get a MacArthur genius grant for this idea.

"Do you need some help?" the concierge asks as I *boing, boing* past her desk.

"Under control," I tell her just seconds before falling in a heap at the elevator banks. I pick myself up with slow determination, mindful of her eyes on me, and when the elevator opens, I manage to shamble into the cabin with some small measure of self-respect. Dusty, who's now justifiably concerned about any close proximity to my unsteady 190-pound bulk, doesn't want to follow, but I pull him forcibly in after me.

We make it into the room—I even contrive to brush my teeth—and then I bounce over to the bed and topple into it. I'm too tired to put Dusty in his crate. "Keep an eye on things, as long as you're up," I mutter to him as I douse the light. "If anyone calls, just get their number."

And then I'm out.

CHAPTER 18

A Rum Business

When I awaken the next morning, my ankle is still throb-bing and so is my head. Fortunately, my clothes are right on the floor where I left them last night, so I can just pour myself right back into them.

I've got a long day ahead of me so I'd better eat something. Unfortunately, the idea of food is suddenly repulsive. The only thing I can stand is one of those grim little breakfast bars that come wrapped in foil. I always keep a few in my overnight bag just in case of an emergency—and by emergency I mean one of those situations you hear about on the news where a car goes over a railing and lands in such a way as to trap the driver for days so that he has to survive by eating his own foot or some-thing. I've vowed that this will never happen to me. Accordingly, I travel with enough packaged goods to keep me alive, if not happy, for several weeks. I never really thought to consume any of it voluntarily, and munching on the bland, sticky breakfast bar now, I wonder if I wouldn't be better off feasting on my instep.

The day at Uihlein Soccer Park goes more smoothly than the one before. The saga of the Aussie attack is on hold, as the matter has gone to the mysterious "committee." Meanwhile Dee's attention is happily diverted by winning a MACH; i.e., a Master Agility Championship. (A MACH requires 750 points and twenty excellent-class double Qs, which means qualifying in both standard and jumpers on the same day. It gets tougher after that; the requirements double—1,500 points and forty double Qs—for your second MACH; triple for your third; and so on.) This is like Olympic gold for agility trainers and comes with a special baton (it looks like a decorated weave pole) that you wave in the air as you make a victory lap around the ring with your dog, while the crowd gives you a standing ovation. It's Dee's second MACH this year, and I think her ninth overall. But she's much more excited by the fact that Marilyn has aced both her runs today— meaning, she explains to me as if to a child (clearly she knows me well), "If she does the same tomorrow, she earns her first MACH."

On a slightly less exalted note, Dusty's runs are at least faster today, which slightly makes up for the sharp discomfort I endure by running him on a twisted ankle. Marilyn points out afterward that his tail was even wagging the whole time. I chalk it up to increased familiarity with the facility. The shock of the place has worn off. Maybe by tomorrow he'll be ready to Q—something I'd really like. Really, really like. Not that I'm letting myself get too emotionally whipped up for it, but I would in fact consider it empirical proof of the existence of God.

*   *   *

After the day's runs, the All Fours gang heads out to dine at yet another destination offering the delicacies associated with suburban sprawl—the Cheesecake Factory. Gus and Deb have officially adopted me, insisting on once again driving me to dinner (unsurprising given my inebriated state at the end of our meal last night). The suburbs are utterly mystifying to me; every stretch of road looks exactly the same. Gus assures us he recalls the route from last year—then proceeds to take us along a series of dimly lit side streets and commercial drives that seem to spiral off into nowhere. After a while I begin to doubt the wisdom of having placed myself in his hands, while Deb steps in to question more vocally every single turn he makes.

And then all of a sudden, like a beacon, there it is splayed out before us: the Cheesecake Factory, jutting grandly from some Habitrail-like shopping mall. I heave a sigh; we've reached civilization! Or at least a reasonable approximation thereof. I make a mental note: always trust Gus.

Turns out we're the first of our group to arrive, and since the hostess won't seat us until our entire party is here, we stand aside and gab as we wait for the others. Our chatter dries up after twenty minutes, at which time we realize we're still alone. "Where the hell is everybody?" Gus asks. He asks again three minutes later. And then three minutes after that.

After last night I promised myself not to rely on alcohol to get through any social insecurity, but since the embers of my hangover are beginning to flare up again, I decide to allow myself just a *little* hair of the dog. "Anybody care for a drink?" I ask. Turns out neither Gus nor Deb imbibe. I don't let that put me off. I go to the bar and order a mojito. I like a good mojito. This one is fine, if a little sugary. It goes down a bit quickly though. So what the hell, I order another.

Eventually our colleagues straggle in, all with the same look of relief at having finally located the place. Looking over the endless menu, I realize the Cheesecake Factory is one of those something-for-everybody joints that offer dishes from every imaginable cuisine. I swallow my compulsion to quip about a restaurant that purports to prepare Chinese chicken salad and spaghetti carbonara with equal measures of expertise. In an effort to play it safe, I order another steak (after securing a bottle of A1) and congratulate myself on my forbearance in not announcing my sacrifice to all and sundry. After all, drawing attention to myself as a gourmand in the wilds of suburban Wisconsin probably won't win me any points. And more important, I'm here for the camaraderie, not the food.

Noticing that Dee and Marilyn are still missing, I order another mojito to help pass the time. I vow it will be the last. Inhibitions dissolved, I find my hand straying into Gus and Deb's nachos. Soon my fingers are greasy, my mustache flecked with avocado, and I'm laughing at things that aren't really funny. I've sailed into dangerous waters.

Dee and Marilyn eventually arrive, having first mistakenly gone to an entirely different Cheesecake Factory on the opposite side of town. What this says about exurban America is something Tocqueville might have foreseen. I resist the urge for another mojito to help me contemplate it.

Awed and impressed by my willpower, I allow myself a cele-

bratory glass of wine with my steak. It's not a mojito, so techni-
cally I'm not breaking my vow. What I *am* breaking, however, is
the cardinal rule of middle age, which is "Do not mix." Had I not
done this, had I just stuck with rum, I would've been all right. But
oh no. I had to go and live on the edge, didn't I?

From here on it all becomes a blur. I don't remember getting
back to the hotel, don't remember walking Dusty, don't remember going to bed.

I will never, however, forget the wake-up call the next
morning—the soulless drone of the electronic voice: "It is now.
Seven. Thirty. Good morning." I feel as if some fascist lodged in
my skull were using my brainpan as a gong. I try to sit up, but the
room goes all Tilt-A-Whirl and I have to lie back down again. I
slowly turn my head—it feels like it's going to fall off and roll
across the floor—and there's Dusty perched on the other bed,
looking at me with, I swear, one eyebrow cocked. It may not be a
judgmental look, but if not, it's a withholding-judgment look.

"Judge not, lest ye be judged," I croak. Then I realize he soon
will be judged, and unlike me he won't have the excuse of exces-
sive alcohol to bolster any failure. "So you'd better step up to the
plate," I add, wagging a finger wanly at him. "Or we'll both be going home with egg on our face."

The thought of eggs makes me alternately hungry and nause-
ated, and I head hastily to the bathroom not knowing which im-
perative will win out.

CHAPTER 19

One for the Team

The cold rips through me like a rusty saw, while the sun reflects off the snow with cruel brilliance. Everything is too sharp, too intrusive, too intense. My hangover worsens with each step toward the car. I imagine the earth suddenly opening at my feet and swallowing me whole. The thought is comforting.

I moan audibly as I drive to Uihlein Park, hunched over the steering wheel like an octogenarian in spinal crisis. My head is absolutely banging. "I am never, ever touching alcohol again as long as I live," I say aloud. I make this same vow several times a year. I'm awfully good with resolution, not so much with the follow-through.

The roar within the facility is very nearly deafening. Like four hundred Bulgarian women's choirs singing all at once. With their dogs. It's as if someone is driving a meat cleaver into my skull, prying it out and sinking it back in again. The small talk at the All Fours crating area feels like firecrackers being lobbed at my head. It's going to be a looooong day.

My jumpers walk-through comes as a welcome respite from the chatter. Though really it's more of a wander-through. I drift semi-consciously, like a spirit in the Greek underworld. Only it's not the waters of the Lethe I've sipped, it's too goddamn much Havana Club.

After the judge's briefing, I get a can of Coke from a vending machine and drink it down like mother's milk. I know it's a drug. My massage therapist is horrified by caffeine in any incarnation. In his opinion, I might as well just ingest plutonium. But he's not here to apply his thumbs to my spine and set me right, and this can of syrupy wide-awake is. I make no apologies. Also, it's hard to worry about the toxicity of a can of cola after the small fermented ocean I sucked up last night.

As if to flaunt his own physical prowess in comparison to my own disabling feebleness, Dusty gives a good run. He stays with me, goes where I tell him to go, keeps a steady pace, doesn't let the judge's proximity spook him, and if not for one too many refusals, we'd actually have had a Q. He's done well; I'm proud of him. He seems to know it, and all but prances off the course like a Clydesdale.

I myself totter and stumble after him, a complete wreck. Just this slight burst of physical activity has dramatically worsened the symptoms of my hangover. Also, my ankle's flaring up again. I'd almost forgotten about it till now, the way you no longer notice a hangnail when you're being impaled on a pike.

I'd like nothing more than to slump down in my chair and put my mind on hold, but I'm fatally distracted by low, excited voices from just a few steps away. A few of the All Fours women are huddled together, furiously whispering. From what I overhear, it seems while I was busy with my run Marilyn racked up another Q in jumpers—which means, with her next run she could earn a MACH. This is admittedly exciting, and I'm guessing from everyone's furtive behavior that no one wants to jinx it (kind of the way pro baseball players won't utter a word while one of their teammates is pitching a no-hitter).

The nervous anticipation starts to get under my skin and my head throbs anew. It's no good staying here—I'll have to go to my car to get any rest. With the heat amped up, I fall into a deep slumber. When I awaken almost half an hour later there's drool running down my chin. There's not a dog in the place who's not more sophisticated than I am. I'm also in full view of anyone who walks by my windshield. I can't help wondering how many people have glanced in at me and then moved along slowly shaking their heads.

After a stop at the All Fours snack table (where I wolf down almost an entire bag of pretzels and can't remember anything ever tasting so good—a point I vocalize repeatedly so that people begin to smile nervously, in a "dude, they're just pretzels" kind of way), I head out for my novice standard run.

And what do you know, it's entirely respectable. The teeter remains our perennial stumbling block, but everything else is as nicely executed as I could ask for. It seems I was right, increasing familiarity with this place has eased Dusty's anxiety and boosted his performance. We don't Q, but it seems churlish to complain, as we've not only enjoyed ourselves but strengthened our rapport.

Back at the crating area, I keep Dusty out with me. Two days ago this would have been a penance for him, not a reward. He's visibly more relaxed than he's ever been before. At one point he inches over to the crate where Cyndi's boxers are sleeping and gives it a few curious sniffs. Cyndi, who's seated right there telling a story, unconsciously lets her arm drop and the tips of her fingers graze Dusty's back. She's actually stroking him. He's actually *letting* her. I look around to see if anyone else is picking up on this Kodak moment, but no, it's just me.

A few moments later, Dusty turns and trots back to me, perfectly contented. I feel like having a party. *This* is a breakthrough! I realize it's possible he's picked up on my own increased ease and self-confidence among these people. After spending forty-eight hours straight with them, I really feel at home with everyone here. I almost wish we were coming back tomorrow, but alas I've got a family obligation.

There's no time to dwell on it, as Dee is in our midst now, ushering us to get to our feet—it's time for Marilyn's standard run. You can almost hear the collective intake of breath; everyone knows a MACH is at stake here.

Marilyn is on the line with River. Both look cool, poised, and confident. Marilyn puts River in a sit-stay and then takes a *huge* lead out. Seriously, she just keeps walking. For a moment I wonder whether she's actually heading out to get a burger or something. Finally, she turns and calls River over the first jump. River takes it with a shrug—almost like it's beneath her notice. From there Marilyn calls her through the tire, and then up the dog walk. Even on the mezzanine I can hear the clatter of River's nails as she gallops across the planks.

After another pair of jumps, they veer off to the left toward the A-frame, which River ascends like she's got pistons in her back end. Marilyn waits for her on the downside, to make sure she doesn't fly off too soon. After River touches down she looks up at Marilyn, as if to say, "How's that?" It's just a heartbeat, but it's endearing, a sign of a team that's really wired in to each another. Then they're off and running again, clearing two more jumps.

So far the course doesn't seem so fiendish. In fact Marilyn's had River on her right the entire time, not even needing to front cross. But now comes a harrowing moment, as they face two successive jumps almost parallel to each other, requiring the dog to sketch the most slender S. Marilyn not only keeps River on her right, but astonishingly leads her over these jumps from several steps *ahead*. My jaw drops: what kind of crazy-ass telepathy have they got going on down there?

Then a sharp left to the teeter—and by sharp I mean you-could-shear-a-leg-off sharp—and Marilyn finally front crosses to get River on her left. It's so smoothly executed I almost don't see it—they're just suddenly reversed. Like teleportation or a trick with mirrors.

Another jump and then onto the table. River's having a good time now, throwing herself around like a rag doll. On the table she gives a good shake, as if to remind herself that this is serious business, and then lies down at Marilyn's command.

Not a muscle is moved during the judge's countdown. Five and four and three and two and *go*. River shoots up like a bottle rocket and Marilyn guides her into a tunnel curled under the dog walk. Another front cross and right into the chute; wow, that tunnel-chute combo has to be disorienting. Yet when River bursts forth, she's got a smile on her face and Marilyn is already waiting for her at the next jump.

Another front cross—they're coming too fast for me to track now—and another jump. Suddenly, the weave poles seem to spring up out of nowhere. Instead of colliding into them, River threads her way through like a lock of hair through a comb. Another front cross, another whiplash turn, another jump—wait, where are they? I have to grasp the railing to keep my balance— and suddenly the crowd is cheering, shrieking, flapping its arms as if to signal a passing plane.

Marilyn and River are off on their victory lap, without even waiting to be awarded the official MACH wand. River takes the weave poles again, almost as though she's showing off: "You really thought that was tough? Watch, I'll do it again."

There's a mass exodus back to the crating area, where Dee is ready with cards and gifts and cake, and Marilyn and River are feted like, well, champions. But to me the surprising element is that every member of the All Fours team seems as invested in this victory as Marilyn herself. Actually, Marilyn appears a bit more reserved about it than the rest. It's clearly a catharsis, something each of us can share—the high point of our weekend. Even more surprising, I feel a part of this victory too. That's how communities work, I guess. I'm learning; I'm learning.

The group's solidarity is further displayed in what will turn out, for me, to be an even more satisfying moment. Diane, who's been fighting an uphill battle with Annie for three days straight, finally finishes a course with her, in decent form and time. We're all there watching, once again holding our breath, and the look on Diane's face when she crosses the finish line—a kind of mixture of exhilaration and sweet relief—is something I'll carry with me a long time. We're all there to howl with approval. There are different kinds of triumph; today I've seen two.

It's getting dark now and I've got to hit the road. But it's hard to walk out on a party in progress, and that's exactly what's going on back at the crating area. As I pack up Dusty's crate, I'm entreated to stay just a few hours longer. "We're going out for Mexican," Dee says enthusiastically. "Dollar-ninety-nine margaritas!"

Something inside me shudders and quakes, and my thirty-year détente with regurgitation almost comes to an ignoble end. I don't want to admit that in my current state alcohol is probably the single greatest disincentive on the planet, so instead I say, "I wish I could, but I've got a ninety-minute drive ahead of me, and I don't want to put it off."

"You can always leave first thing tomorrow," says Betsy.

"Actually, I can't. I've already checked out of my hotel."

My regrets are regretfully accepted. I take my leave. And the celebration goes on without me. I feel heavy with real regret; cheap margaritas aside, this was a party I'd have liked to be part of. As we zip through the crisp cold night, it feels like my family obligation is calling me away from, well, a family obligation.

CHAPTER 20

Polarized

There's something about extreme temperatures that freezes up my facility for language. All I can think, as I mute the alarm and throw back the covers, is, "Cold. Cold. Damn, damn, damn, it's cold." I'm suddenly about as articulate as the Incredible Hulk. And as sweet tempered.

I dress in a hurry. I should probably shower; I didn't shower yesterday, and certainly the idea of standing under jets of hot water is an attractive one. Not so, however, the idea of stepping back out into an icy bathroom, dripping wet, steam wafting off me in sheets as all the heat jumps ship. So I'll pass on the personal hygiene, thanks. Besides, I'm going to a big barn filled with dogs. No matter how rank I am, no one's going to notice.

Fried eggs for breakfast. I put some of the egg white on Dusty's food—this is the secret, I've discovered, to getting him to eat before a trial. Got to surprise him with novelty. Sort of like having an eternal two-year-old. I turn around to present the bowl to him, and he's not there.

Ah.

Damn.

He's anticipated what's coming—a long drive and a day of noise and confusion—and he's retreated into his crate.

Now, I have a long-standing rule about crates. They're my dogs' "safe space." This is particularly useful when they arrive at the house for the first time. While they're in their crates, no one will bother them. It eases their insecurities during the period when they're adjusting to the new routine, absorbing the new smells, and learning the new environment. In fact my dogs find such comfort in their crates that I leave them up and open even after they're fully acclimated to the life of the house. They enjoy periodically retreating there to relax or nap.

But now Dusty's gone and taken refuge in his, like a thief taking sanctuary in a church. And he *will not come out*. I command him, I plead, I bribe—I even grab our pet parakeet, whose feathery goodness he has long wanted to sample, and dangle the terrified bird by the crate door, hoping Dusty won't be able to resist taking a lunge.

But no. He's on to me. He won't budge for the budgerigar. He looks at me with eyes that suddenly seem so very unreadable, so animal, so *other*.

"Look, buddy," I say. "I don't particularly want to go myself. It's three below zero and, yeah, I'd rather stay in bed. I'd rather stay there till freakin' April. But we have responsibilities here. We have obligations. Come on now. Come. Dusty, *come*."

Uh-uh. He presses even farther against the back grid and sort of folds himself flat, like origami.

And that's when I do it. Overcome by fatigue and cold and, well, *cold*, I reach into the crate, grab his collar, and haul him out.

Is it my imagination, or does his face register stunned betrayal? Or is it just my own shock I've projected onto his? I can't believe what I just did. I've broken a sacred trust. This can never be undone.

So now in addition to the bone-biting cold, I've got guilt clinging to me like a clammy sheet. Oh, this weekend is starting out beautifully. To what depths will I descend from here? Maybe I'll have struck him by the end of the day or have left him by the side of the road with no cab fare.

I try to put it out of my mind as we head out onto the deck. It's so cold that the planks creak like gunshots as we cross them. God, I *despise* this kind of weather. Why on earth did I book a trial for the end of January, anyway? What the hell was I thinking?

I know exactly what I was thinking. I'd been talking to Dee about the pros and cons of various facilities, and the Rush 'N' Around Agility Center in Manhattan came up. Not one of her favorites, as it happens: she doesn't like the turf (I never bothered looking at it myself, but I don't tell her that). I mentioned that I'd run Dusty there a few months earlier and Q'd, and she said, "Oh, if I Q'd there I'd be back every week."

So I went home and dutifully booked the next available trial there, forgetting that it's basically a big, open pole barn. I just forged right ahead and got on the roster, without considering how hard it must be to heat a place like that. Now I'm paying the price for my damn-the-torpedoes approach to ribbon hunting.

It's so cold my car's engine sasses back to me for a few nasty moments, arguing against my desire to ignite it. But eventually it gives in—with a final, rather graceless shudder—and I immediately dial the heat up to sixty-eight degrees. The sooner this cabin goes tropical, the better.

I'm far too uncomfortable to work up the focus required for orchestral or even chamber music, so I put on something lighter: June Christy's *Something Cool*, from way back in 1955. It's one of the very first concept albums, a suite of jazz songs designed to evoke a languid, torpid summer day. As I drive through the frigid dark of predawn Chicago, I try to imagine myself in the place the music wants to take me: a stinging sun overhead, sweat on my brow, my shirt sticking to my back, the heat of the sidewalk seeping up through my shoes. It's hard work, but I'm motivated, and by the time we reach Manhattan—a few unlovely eruptions on the otherwise barren landscape—I'm actually driving comfortably with my gloves off.

But now I've got to put them back on and head into the facility. To my surprise, there aren't more then two dozen cars here. I'd expected a hundred. True, the trial is novice and open only, but it's also offering FAST and I thought that might draw a crowd. Could the brain-splitting cold have kept some competitors home? Why didn't I think of that?

As I feared, it's only slightly warmer inside, so I keep my hat and gloves on. In fact I'm wearing two hats. I must look like the village idiot.

There's a hush over the place. Even the dogs aren't making more than a few token whines and growls. The vibe is very much post-apocalyptic. It wouldn't surprise me to see people start a fire and roast one of the larger hounds. Or one of the smaller handlers.

I see a few familiar faces, among them Vicky Bruning with her Sheltie, Dakota, and a handsome Belgian Tervuren as well. I nod and exchange a few words with her, admire her dogs (they really are beauties), but I'm really not feeling social. Hell, I'm not feeling respiratory. I set up Dusty's crate and deposit him inside, then open my collapsible chair and collapse into it.

The reason we're here so early is to try our hand at FAST. Due to increased demand, Dee recently held a special FAST seminar in place of our usual Thursday class. It turns out that FAST has nothing to do with speed. Instead it's an acronym for "fifteen and send time." The basic idea is that each obstacle has a point value from one to ten (which is denoted by the cone sitting next to it), and each handler is free to run the course in whatever way he or she thinks will best accrue them. You need a certain number of points to qualify; in novice, it's fifty.

Sounds easy. But there's one major wrinkle: at some point during your run, you have to do what's called the "send bonus." This comprises either a single obstacle or a combination of two or three. The good news is that you get twenty additional points for completing it. The bad news is that you have to guide your dog through it from a distance of four or five feet (hence the term *send*). The even worse news is, if you don't finish the send bonus, you don't qualify. And you get only one shot; you can't retry it.

This is our first attempt at FAST, and I'm not expecting great things. Dusty's not very good at distance work. I can't really successfully send him to anything except the exit. All the same, FAST intrigues me because I can tailor a run that avoids the obstacles he has the most difficulty with. So in theory it allows me to play to our strengths and increases our chances of qualifying.

Of course, it's about twenty-eight degrees on the course, and as I walk it, trying to plot my strategy, I find myself less interested in qualifying than in regaining feeling in my lower extremities. But I figure what the hell, I'm here, I'll butch it up. "Butch it up" is one of those wonderfully self-motivating phrases. Just saying it aloud somehow buoys you. Suddenly I feel lean. I feel limber. I feel ready to rumble.

Dusty, however, is sluggish and distracted. I can understand: he's much, much smaller than I am, and in this cold his blood must have the consistency of a Slurpee. But as I said, we're here, we'll butch it up. I try the phrase on him, but mentally he's back in the crate I so rudely yanked him out of this morning. The way his shoulders are hunched bespeaks his wariness and distrust of me. I might as well be wearing a big rubber Freddy Krueger mask.

All the same, our run goes well. There's a dodgy bit at the beginning where Dusty seems too fascinated by the turf, which, I now see, is a kind of shredded rubber mulch. (It's as unappealing as it sounds, I assure you. It looks disturbingly like larvae and I can only imagine how it smells to canine nostrils. I can understand why Dee considers it a liability.) But I manage to snap him out of it, and then he shakes off his sulkiness and becomes very nearly spry. Even better, when I direct him to the send bonus—which is a tunnel-tire combination—he actually goes for it. He dives admirably into the tunnel and shoots out the other side like a spitball, and I'm already writing my "brags" e-mail in my head when he unaccountably and infuriatingly ducks under the tire instead of going through it.

That's it—that's my game ender right there. I finish the run, trying to sound as cheerful as possible, but without the send bonus, it all means nothing. We've NQ'd. A seventy-minute drive in antarctic conditions to get here at daybreak, and it's all been for sweet Fanny Adams.

Well, there's always tomorrow.

In the little time before our standard run, I take Dusty back to the car and sit there, hoping to warm up. Unfortunately, on a day like this the little heating unit really isn't up to the task of beating back Mother Nature's icy grip. The dashboard shoots a stream of warm air at me, but it's laced with the frigid seepage from the car's many seams; they may be watertight, but this cold is more insidious than any mere liquid. It oozes through gaps at the molecular level. Dusty curls up in the backseat, tucking his snout beneath his tail, looking much like a stole.

Something Cool has jingled back to life with the engine, so I drop back against the headrest and concentrate on listening to it over the roar of the air vents. I've loved this album since my college days. It was the first collaboration between Christy and Pete Rugolo, the arranger-conductor of all her finest albums, which followed fast and furious after this one: *The Misty Miss Christy* in 1956, *Fair and Warmer* and *Gone for the Day* in 1957, *The Song Is June!* and *This Is June Christy!* in 1958, *Those Kenton Days* in 1959, and *Off Beat* in 1960—culminating in a complete rerecording, this time in stereo, of *Something Cool* in 1960.

This CD release, in fact, features both the mono and stereo versions on one disc. I amuse myself by playing each 1955 cut followed by its 1960 analogue. Subtle differences in tempo, phrasing, and orchestration suddenly appear much more profound.

It occurs to me that this is possibly extreme behavior. It occurs to me, as well, that there are probably very few people living who know as much about the June Christy discography as I do. Even fewer who could, extemporaneously, argue the merits of her various conductors. (Rugolo is tops, of course, but then what of Stan Kenton, in whose band she achieved stardom? Or her husband, Bob Cooper, who conducted the devastating *Ballads for Night People?*)

Looking out the window, across the vast expanse of fallow fields under a sky of gunmetal gray, I wonder if anyone within fifty miles of this place even knows who June Christy is. I wonder, too, whether the strains of any of the songs on this disc have ever sounded in these parts, and if so, how long ago.

Then my perspective shifts and the vehicles around me come into focus. They're all vans, I notice (I'm the only moron here with a sports car), with crates loaded in the back and agility-themed bumper stickers and back windows bedecked with blue ribbons. No, I correct myself, *this* is extreme behavior. After all, I don't have a June Christy bumper sticker. I don't even listen to June Christy more than two or three times a year. It's just a quirk of my personality that I gather information the way furniture collects lint. But *these* people—they're hard-core. They're here in the kind of cold you usually find only on the fringe of the solar system, pursuing this ridiculously irrelevant endeavor and loving it. And as much as I try to be one of them, I can't. It was foolish ever to have thought I could; I was doomed to failure before I started. I'm too distracted by other ideas, other thoughts, other interests. I'm too fatally aware of *context*.

In a way, I envy these people. It must be nice to have such a thorough, down-to-the-bone knowledge of one *big* thing, instead of little smatterings of knowledge about everything. The latter may make me an amusing dinner guest, but I'll never really belong anywhere like these people belong here.

I find myself recalling a recent All Fours session at which Dee surprised us with a video she'd put together: a thirty-minute, post-MACH tribute to Marilyn and River, composed of footage of them in competition going back years (with the requisite soundtrack; i.e., Queen's "We Are the Champions" and the like).

My initial reaction was genuine surprise that Marilyn hasn't always been as supremely elegant a performer as she is now. The footage of her earlier runs revealed a rougher-edged competitor, more prone to mistakes and miscues. It was both surprising and gratifying to see her make some of the goofs I myself commit on a regular basis. Also, in some of the more recent footage she was miked, so even though she looked on the surface to be breezing through a spotlessly clean run, you could hear the tremor in her commands, the nervousness and determination, the grit. I once read an essay on Fred Astaire that described the hours of grueling rehearsal behind his seemingly effortlessness dance routines. It seems this is true of Marilyn as well. The naked eye sees swiftness, sureness, ease; while, underneath, the furnace is stoked and blazing.

But then I felt another reaction come over me: one of surprising numbness. Seeing Marilyn's entire agility history edited together this way—all those dozens of runs melding into each other like dreams—I feel the cumulative effect of witnessing many, many variations on a very restricted set of possibilities. Jump, weave, jump, tunnel, tire, frame; a change of scenery, then chute, jump, jump, dog walk, jump, weave. A new locale, then tunnel, tire, jump, jump, jump, frame, weave—and so on, without pause or respite.

Sitting here now, in this bleak terrain, beneath a chalky sky, I see nothing ahead of me but this kind of whirling sameness, increasing in speed and intensity, like water spiraling down a drain.

But this is silliness. I'm letting a little exhaustion and discomfort turn into something inappropriately melodramatic. Best just to put the whole business right out of my mind.

I turn off the engine, open the door, and a gust of polar wind slams into me like a truck. I go momentarily numb and consider how easy it would be to just shut the door again and drive back home.

But no, not now. Not now. We've got our standard run.

So I hook up Dusty, and go in to run it.

CHAPTER 21

Bloodied and Bowed

Sunday dawns. The second day of the trial. Even colder than the first. As soon as I throw back the covers, my will to live is atomized.

I force myself out of bed, but even so I wonder, "What's the point?" We finished out yesterday with more refusals than a Catholic girls' school on prom night. Dusty bailed on the teeter, balked at the tire, shirked the A-frame, ducked the jumps, fled the weave poles, snubbed the table, and dodged the dog walk. The only thing he did, and did consistently, was the tunnel. Maybe it was warmer in there.

He doesn't want to go back, and I don't either. But I remind myself of the champions in this world; they're the people with the spirit to persist, who strive against defeat and dismay (and probably cold too, though they never seem to mention that) and end up achieving something magnificent. Maybe if we stick it out, that'll be us too. Maybe this will be our day. Maybe this will be the turning point, the harbinger of future glory. Maybe I am Queen Marie of Romania.

As I dress myself, I consider the odds. Our best shot remains the FAST session that leads off the day. I can't let myself get dispirited about Dusty blowing the send bonus yesterday; it was the first time he'd ever encountered one. In view of which, he did very well. He *almost* Q'd. Today maybe he actually will.

When we arrive at the trial, the first thing I learn is that the send bonus is jump-teeter. I heave a dejected sigh. Easy come, easy goddamn go.

As it turns out, the send bonus doesn't even get the opportunity to trip us up. Dusty's so distracted on the course that we're whistled off after tackling just two obstacles. He won't look at me, won't listen to me, keeps running the perimeter of the ring and smiling at spectators, like a member of the royal family on walkabout. I actually have to pick him up and tote him off the course under my arm. We pass right by a big trash can, and, boy, am I tempted to stop and lighten my load.

We've got a long wait till our standard run, but I now know better than to try to warm up in the car; it'll only make me feel that much colder when I return. Also, every time I reenter the facility, my glasses fog up, and it seems to take forever for them to clear. (I used a handkerchief to wipe them yesterday, but that only succeeded in smearing the fog around.)

So today I'll just stay put and let my body accustom itself to the temperature inside this big sheet-metal box. Dusty will be fine in his crate; he's got a dish of water and I've given him a biscuit on the odd chance he'll actually want one. He ate nothing this morning, too busy sulking at the way I'd preemptively shut the door to his crate so he couldn't stage another "hell no, I won't go" move.

As for me, I've brought along a backlog of "Dining In" sections from the Wednesday *New York Times*—months' worth that I've been meaning to get around to. This seems like the perfect time and place. I begin plowing through them, particularly delighted, as usual, by Mark Bittman's column, "The Minimalist." It's a minor miracle the way he continually comes up with recipes comprising just a few scant ingredients that, with the alchemy of a little mixing or a little heat, transform into something sublime. I'm just salivating over his column on short ribs braised in coffee when a woman sidles up to me and begins to talk.

I've always found this a bit irritating—this assumption, which pretty much everyone in our postliterate society seems to make, that the act of reading is something we undertake only out of boredom and from which we are desperate to be rescued by any interruption whatsoever—but I've long since given up displaying any righteous indignation. No one ever picks up on it. Besides, I was just yesterday envying these people, bemoaning how I didn't fit in with them, so I can scarcely get my nose out of joint when one of them actually decides to talk to me.

Plus, let's face it, I'm just reading a recipe, not freakin' Schopenhauer.

"I noticed you running your Sheltie," says the woman—fiftysomething, very round; the shape Jeffrey and I call "globe" (*pace* E. F. Benson). "She seems very nervous around the judge."

"Does he?" I reply, pointedly inserting the correct pronoun without further comment (something dog owners have to do a lot). "I suppose he is. He's certainly always aware of the judge's whereabouts."

"Oh, you don't have to tell me! I've got a Sheltie of my own, and she's *hyperaware* of the judge. Also the timekeepers, the bar setter, the photographer . . . I don't want to offend your politics, but we always say she's a Republican: she sees terrorists everywhere."

I laugh; it's a funny line. We commiserate about the shyness of our dogs a bit longer; then she drifts slowly away, like the moon.

I return to "The Minimalist," but at just about this time someone starts serving up sloppy joes to the volunteers. And suddenly I am yanked rudely from the culinary paradise of Mark Bittman into a kind of greasy hell. What can I say, I grew up in an Italian household; food, to me, is sacred and its preparation the focal point of each day. For my people, cooking and eating are the twin rituals that give the rest of life its meaning. And the way these people here are dishing up this toxic sludge and slapping it onto some spongy substance passing as bread simply assails my senses.

I put up with this same aromatic onslaught when I competed here several months ago, but then the barn doors were open and plenty of fresh air was rolling in to dilute it. Also, I wasn't then cringing in discomfort from the inability to feel the cheeks on which I was sitting, as is the case now. It all feeds the tendency to tetchiness.

The only thing for it is to get up and go outside till I can regain my equilibrium. Presuming I can manage to do that in conditions that can make small birds fall dead out of the sky. I go and fetch Dusty and hook him up—pausing only to notice that the water in his dish has frozen—and lead him out the door. I'll look much more natural standing out there attached to a dog than I would all by myself, muttering darkly and stamping sensation back into my feet. Also, you never know, Dusty might actually like to move his bowels again one of these days. If only for the novelty value.

As we pass by a clutch of people, I hear a familiar voice saying, "not to offend your politics, but we always say she's a Republican: she looks for terrorists everywhere." I can't exactly say why, but this utterly depresses me. It's like nothing can even bother to stay fresh anymore.

When we get outside it's nearly blinding, the midday sun reflecting mercilessly on the snow. Other people are out cavorting with their dogs, frolicking and galumphing and having a swell old time despite the temperature's almost double-digit deficit. Dusty just looks at me through the steam of breath that shrouds his head like Vesuvius and arches one eyebrow, as if to say, "What's wrong with you?"

It's a question I should be asking myself. I'm feeling snarky, unsettled, misanthropic. I'm not even concentrating on the other competitors, which I usually do, on the principle that you *can* learn from other people's mistakes. I'm in the middle of nowhere, making a very good show of being a dilettante, for the benefit of no one in particular.

Someone passes behind us and Dusty astonishes me by whirling around and nearly tearing off the ear of a giant bullmastiff. Fortunately, I'm able to rein him in at the critical moment, so he doesn't even graze the larger dog's fur; but the mastiff's owner is, understandably, a bit put out. "C'mon, Cody," he says. "Give the pipsqueak some space."

"Sorry!" I call after him, and he waves dismissively as he reenters the barn. Then I turn to Dusty and say, "What the hell's wrong with you?" Which, it occurs to me, is more or less the attitude he's taken with me.

Suddenly it occurs to me: Snarky? Unsettled? Misanthropic? I'm describing Dusty! How many times do I have to learn this lesson? My dog's pathologies are of my own making. He takes his cues from me, and my cues this weekend have been pretty unmistakable: We don't want to be here. We don't belong here. We're angry at the world and we want to be left alone. God, I've gone and created a mini-me on four legs.

All right, then. Got to take a deep breath and shift gears radically. Set aside my discomfort, my pettiness, my navel-gazing, and focus on the task at hand. Got to *butch it up*. And all this—the cold, the smelly turf, the smellier food—these are the kind of problems champions thrive on overcoming. It's about time we prove we *are* champions.

We head back inside, and my glasses immediately fog up. But not even this dims my iron resolve. "Come on, boy," I tell Dusty as I lead him, half-blind, back to the ring. "Let's rock and roll!"

Unfortunately, we end up string-quartetting. Dusty's energy level is still way down, and while he takes a few jumps, he skirts enough of the others to make the whole endeavor largely meaningless. Still, I've only just reframed my attitude; possibly it'll take a bit longer for him to get the new vibe.

In the meantime, I've got just enough time to wolf down my own lunch before our standard run. I've left a pancetta-and-buffalo-mozzarella panino in the car, and after returning Dusty to his chilly little crate, I head back outside to get it.

This time I decide to play it smart and just remove my glasses before exiting. If they're in my pocket, they won't get cold enough to fog up when I get back. I'm amazed by the brilliance of this idea, and it irks me I didn't think of it yesterday.

Just as I'm reaching for the knob, the door swings open—and because I don't have my glasses on I can't see it in time to avoid it. The edge hits me square in the face. For a moment I hear the chirping of little birds, like the Three Stooges do when clobbered. "Oh, hey, I'm sorry," someone says. "You all right, buddy?"

"I'm fine, I'm fine," I say as I blink, trying to make him out; but of course without my glasses all I see is a big blob of pink and gray.

"You sure about that?" He puts a hand on my shoulder to steady me. At least he's a *well-meaning* blob of pink and gray.

"Uh-huh, no problem," I murmur, and then I shimmy by him, embarrassed. I don't like being seen at less than my best. It's a guy thing.

I get to the car, scramble into the driver's seat, fumble my glasses out of my jacket, and have a look at my face in the rearview mirror. Blood is *gushing* from my nose. Why didn't my assailant tell me? I'll give him the benefit of the doubt: it's probably hard to see, what with my big black moustache. I look around for some tissues to stanch the flow. There are few ancient, used ones rolled up in the pocket of the door. They feel crispy and cold, like dead insects.

So here I am, sitting in a frigid car in the middle of a barren prairie with my life's blood cascading from me in the most humiliating possible manner. And I have to run my dog in a matter of *minutes*. I tilt my head back, trying to stem the thick, red tide.

Eventually, it slows to a trickle—either that or the cold has just frozen it in place. Whatever, it'll have to do.

I jump out of the car and head back into the barn, stopping in the restroom to daub the worst of the carnage from my facial hair (and to wipe my glasses, which have once more gone all milky). Then I go back to the ring, where the standard walk-through has already begun. I hurry on in and take my place in the throng, and as I'm walking with my arm outstretched, plotting my maneuvers, I can feel the moisture on my moustache start to freeze. It feels like I could reach up and just snap the whole thing off at the roots. Instant clean shave.

After the judge's briefing, I go back to my chair, and as I sit down I notice some flecks of blood on my thighs. And then a few more. The sudden burst of energy has got me bleeding again. By the time I've got it back under control, it's our turn to run. I'm muttering and cursing and people are starting to steer clear of me. I realize I must look absolutely crazy, the guy in two hats growling under his breath and bleeding all over himself.

I grab Dusty and get in the line, really not caring what happens anymore—not even thinking about it. I'm just taking this one moment at a time, putting one foot after the other. Whatever it takes so that I can go home and crawl under some dark, warm covers and go all fetal for the next geologic cycle or so.

And then we're off. I've got to yank Dusty's attention from the turf again; then after few obstacles we're at the weave poles. And Dusty decides to adopt the interesting fiction that he has never seen anything like them before. He circles them, looking at them with his head slightly cocked, as if saying, "I'll be damned, what do you make of these?" I have to work like hell to get him through them, one pole at a time. At one point I even catch myself sputtering, "Dusty, God *damn* it"—first time I've ever cursed him out in the ring, and I can only hope the judge hasn't heard it.

But then he picks up speed and finishes beautifully. And I mean *beautifully*. So much so that I think we may actually have qualified. A single Q would salvage this whole sorry experience. Even better, since there are only three dogs in my jump height, a Q would automatically place. It's been a while since we brought home a ribbon.

I'm feeling almost giddy at the prospect of having snatched victory from the jaws of ignominy. As I wait for the scores to go up, my confidence grows, and I find myself rehearsing the story of the disastrous weekend and its unexpectedly brilliant finish, as though I'm already at a table of rapt dinner guests.

Twenty minutes later the scores are posted. I put on my glasses and run my finger down the listings till I get to the sixteens. I locate Dusty's name—and after it a big NQ. What the hell? How is that possible?

Then I look at the time. Dusty and I clocked in at seventy-one seconds. *Seventy-bloody-one*. A freaking *eternity*. I should've just bought property next to the dog walk and settled down out there.

I storm out in a kind of blind rage. This entire weekend has been an unmitigated disaster, heaping indignity upon indignity, humiliation upon humiliation. The sooner I put it behind me, the better. I pack up the car, throw myself into the driver's seat, shift into drive, and slam my foot on the accelerator.

The engine whines shrilly; the car doesn't move.

What the bloody buggery bollocks is wrong now? I fling open the door and get out, go to the back end, and see that my rear wheels are planted on a large patch of ice. Of all the heinous, ill-timed annoyances.

I look around for anyone nearby who might give me a push; alas, there's not a soul to be seen. Before I endure the embarrassment of going back into the barn to beg the aid of one of the few stragglers, I decide to try kicking some dirt under the wheels, to give them some traction.

The ground is hard and the dirt frozen in place, and all I end up doing is hurting my foot. I lean against the trunk to massage my sore toes, and before I realize what's happening, the pressure of my hand sends the car inching forward, leaving me to fall backward on my bum.

Of all the stupid moves—I've left the car in gear! It's now rolling across the flat, tundralike landscape, the door hanging open and Dusty looking out the rear window with an expression of nascent concern.

I scramble to my feet and give chase, but skidding along the icy ground the car slowly picks up speed. Nothing exceptional—it can't be going much more than ten miles an hour—but it's enough to keep me galloping after it in vain, wildly cursing every deity from Jehovah to Shiva.

Somewhere in the midst of this hideous pursuit, it occurs to me that it's an almost perfect metaphor for my agility career: I keep trying harder and harder, yet my goal pulls ever farther away from me. It seems the universe is trying to tell me something (while having a good laugh at my expense).

Well, fine. Point taken, universe. And by the way, screw you.

I'm gasping for air now—my lungs raked by jagged icicles—when I realize that the car is cruising sedately toward a denuded tree. I don't know whether to be happy or horrified and haven't yet decided when the passenger side makes contact, scraping into the tree trunk and coming to an ugly halt.

A few seconds later, I reach the scene and survey the damage. There's a big, long gouge in the exterior; I wail like a baby seal at the sight of it. Then I feel a spasm of guilt that I've surveyed the car's condition before that of my dog. I peer into the back window and there he is, sitting primly in his seat harness and looking at me in much the way Miss Daisy looked at Hoke when she'd had quite enough of needless delays.

My brow, already slick with cold sweat, fires up in irritation. I'm glad Dusty's fine, of course, but does he have to be *lofty*? Another sign from the cosmos. We're not on the same page, not in the same *book*—we never are. We never were. I sigh and stand upright, and a branch of the tree pokes me right behind my glasses.

Cursing again—and crying too, both from frustration and, excuse me, *ow, my eye*—I walk around the front of the car, realizing as I do that this is a stupid thing to risk. The thing's still in gear, for God's sake. Fortunately, the universe decides I don't actually need to be run over to get the message it's sending me.

I get back inside and slam the door shut. As I buckle up, I become aware of the spatters of viscous blood all over my coat front. I look in the rearview mirror and see that I'm back to gushing like an oil well. The exclamation point on today's epiphany. All right, okay, you win.

I look over my shoulder to where Dusty sits with his head blithely cocked, and tell him, "Okay, boy! That was it! That was your career. You can rest easy now, 'cause it's *over. O-v-e-r.* We are *never* doing this again."

To calm myself for the drive home, I pull a disc at random from the glove box. It's another jazz outing, 1964's *The Lonely Hours* by Sarah Vaughan. Within a few minutes she's woefully wailing:

Friendless, there's not a soul to care
I'm friendless, nobody anywhere . . .
A life of desolation is all I see ahead
And in my desperation I wish that I were dead

I reach over and turn it off. I'm just not in the mood for anything so fucking chipper.

Part Three

CHAPTER 22

The Leash Tugs Both Ways

For a few weeks, I don't even think about it.

In fact I throw myself back into the activities I've so long left neglected. I dust off my chef's hat and cook up a storm, filling the house with extravagant aromas. I go back to swimming three times a week, and am soon up to thirty-two laps—a solid mile. I bone up on my Italian, memorizing poetry by reciting it aloud while walking Dusty and Carmen—the only physical activity we now share.

I also begin an exhaustive trawl through the works of Noël Coward. They've been sitting on my shelf for years, but now I've obtained the perfect complement: a newly released DVD collection of his major plays, as produced by the BBC in the 1980s. Each day I read the text of one of them in the morning, and then watch the corresponding DVD in the afternoon. It immerses me in a bracingly alien world of endless cocktails, dressing for dinner, and giddily casual immorality. Not a dog to be seen. Though there's a moment in act one of *Hay Fever*, when someone in the self-consciously bohemian Bliss clan notices that the family dog, Zoe, hasn't been in for her breakfast, and it's darkly conjectured that she might have fallen into a river (though the housekeeper scoffs at this—"She too wily"). Two acts later, the play ends with the following day's breakfast, and there's not been another word said about Zoe. Did she ever come in, I can't help wondering? Is she all right? And would it kill anyone in this underemployed bunch to go out and throw a ball for her every now and then?

So yes, dogs apparently remain near the top of my hierarchy of priorities, but I no longer associate them reflexively with A-frames, weave poles, qualifying scores, and collapsible furniture. In fact it's a bit surprising how little yesterday's obsession impinges on today's train of thought.

Then one day I'm clicking through my log of TiVo recordings, deleting all the episodes of *Iron Chef* I thought I'd catch up with but now realize I never will, and I come across the AKC Agility Invitational—the national championships, the big event of the year, the one I ridiculously imagined I had a chance of reaching with Dusty. (To make it to the championships, you need six excellent double Qs and four hundred points from the previous year. Me, I barely made it out of novice.) I have to laugh. That sad delusion suddenly seems a lifetime ago.

Before I know it, I find myself pressing Play. I tell myself I'll just watch a few minutes.

The show is hosted by someone named Bob Goen, who presumably I am supposed to recognize; he has that insinuating "here I am again in your living room" demeanor that show business creatures often cultivate. He breathily confesses that he's new to the sport, and then introduces his cohost, Terry Simons, a renowned agility competitor who always seems to be on hand for these broadcasts. I assume he was chosen for his lean, craggy good looks, but despite this he's not a natural on-air talent. For one thing, his voice is very thin and small; he tries to make up for it by SHOUT-ING ALL THE TIME, which only strains him to the breaking point. It's a bit painful to hear. He's also quite stiff with his commentary, relying excessively on a few set phrases like "THIS IS A TEAM WHO CAN TAKE IT ALL!" and you could base a college drinking game on how often he responds to a question with "AB-SOLUTELY!" In addition, someone apparently told him that it's important to smile when on camera, because he never once stops, and the effort takes its toll. By the end of the broadcast, his grin seems to have been fixed by rigor mortis.

As for the rest of the show? Well, the entirety of the finals—in which fifty-seven dogs compete for five top honors (one for each jump height)—has been edited down to an hour; less, when you factor in commercials. So you get to see only a few complete runs, bumped up against each other so that there's barely time to absorb one before the next is under way. Still, those are the lucky teams: pity those who are slighted by having their runs reduced to snip-pets of five or six seconds, then jammed together at the beginning of each segment with a voice-over intoning, "Here are the dogs who ran during the break," as though we're stupid enough to think we're watching this live.

This cut-to-the-bone approach can be unintentionally hilarious, as when Terry Simons talks to the winner of each division: in-depth interviews that last all of eleven seconds. Here's the tran-script of one of them, complete and verbatim:

TERRY: I'M HERE WITH SUZANNE BIRD-
SALL, OUR TWELVE-INCH WINNER TO-
NIGHT! SUZANNE, YOU WERE HERE LAST
YEAR BUT YOU DIDN'T MAKE IT TO THE FI-
NALS! YOU'RE THE WINNER THIS YEAR!
WHAT DID YOU DO TO CHANGE YOUR
STYLE OF HANDLING OR TRAINING?

SUZANNE: We've really worked on our lines,
to get straighter lines and tighter turns.

TERRY: WELL YOU DEFINITELY GOT
STRAIGHTER LINES AND TIGHTER TURNS!
CONGRATULATIONS! BACK TO YOU, BOB!

Still, this is Animal Planet, so you forgive the kind of clunky
production values that might annoy you anywhere else. And the
show is not without interest. The courses are fiendishly difficult
(they were designed by one Karen Paulukaitis, who on the evidence presented here could have a real career in organized sa-
dism), and it's shocking to see how just many of these dogs—the
powerhouses, the elite, the top performers in the sport—drop
bars, pop out of the weave poles too early, dive into the wrong
end of the tunnel, and so on. And what's remarkable is that, in
many cases, I can see exactly what the handlers do wrong. I find
myself saying aloud, "Oh, man, *look* where your butt is pointing!"
or "Whoa, you were too late on that cross!"

Periodically, throughout the hour, the show cuts away from
the competition to little confessional vignettes featuring selected
competitors. One of them—Melody Guiver, the handler of a five-
year-old Bedlington terrier named Scout—says, "You need to be

able to keep your cool. You can't get stressed out. 'Cause you're so excited, going up to the line, you know, you need to keep a level head, focus on what you need to do, and work every obstacle."

I feel a little jolt when she says this, as though I've been stung, or just sat down on a whoopee cushion. It's like she's talking directly to me. She may as well just turn to the camera and say, "And *you* there, sitting on your haunches in Chicago because things didn't go your way, boo-goddamn-hoo, you can just get back up and *try again*. You hear me? Prima donna? Stop fiddling with the remote and listen. Yeah, I'm talkin' to *you*."

Shaken, I go out on the deck and look down at dogs in the yard. The daylight is just starting to fade, but it's been a sun-drenched afternoon and much of the season's ice has melted; a little foretaste of spring to get us through the rest of winter. Carmen sits atop a lingering mound of dirty snow; she always seeks out the highest elevation, as though it confers on her some kind of exalted status. But Dusty is fence-running, barking and spinning, his legs and shanks caked with cold, wet grime. I call his name and he gives me one wild look and then goes off on another tear. All of the calm we'd achieved at Hounds seems to have dissipated with this sudden drought of activity.

It occurs to me that I haven't been giving him enough to do. He simmers with repressed energy until he gets outdoors and then erupts with manic energy. I've told myself he hasn't missed agility—but how would I know that? Do I expect him to grab my car keys and run to the garage? Pull his ribbons off the shelf and start wearing them around the house, like the Order of the Garter?

I summon him again, this time in tones he knows he'd better

not ignore. He clatters up the steps and comes to a screeching halt in front of me, damn near leaving skid marks. He's panting, smiling, filthy—there's grit flecked all the way up to the tips of his ears—and gives me a look that says, "Quick, what is it? I'm busy!"

I look into his eyes. He's itchy, restless, unwilling to stand still beneath my scrutiny. "What is it you want, boy?" I ask.

A moment later, I realize it's not his answer I'm awaiting; it's my own. I dismiss him with a wave and he disappears in a blur, spilling down the steps and back to the fence, where he once more explodes into his Tasmanian devil routine. I turn and go back inside the house.

What is it you want, boy?

There's a leg of lamb in the oven, and the scent of garlic and rosemary suffuses the air. I begin trimming a pound of green beans, occasionally pausing to hitch up my jeans, which hang off my hips from all my recent swimming. As my knife stutters across the cutting board, I keep pace by chanting successive stanzas of Dante's *Paradiso* in a low, steady rhythm. Life is full; life is good.

But what is it you want?

From the yard, a burst of staccato barking. Then the quiet roar of afternoon gives way to the burr of early evening—the seductive hiss of the possible.

I want . . .

I want to go back.

CHAPTER 23

Ifs, Andi, Buts

All right, then. If I'm going to return to agility, I'll need a fresh perspective—something to fan my newfound spark into a competitive flame. It occurs to me that I have an invaluable resource in my teammates. Each of them has his or her own particular history; each has a point of view as individual as my own. Hearing about their struggles and achievements can only inspire and reenergize me.

I decide my best bet is Andi, possibly because she's a lot like those breezy, brainy blonds who glide through Woody Allen movies. She has the same offhand air of self-confidence and speaks her mind so plainly, with an occasional barb of wit, that everything she says brims over with casual authority.

I meet her for lunch at an Italian restaurant a block away from the medical center where she works as an information systems analyst. I drove here through a winter storm—the little hiccough of spring having given way to freezing rain, which turned to pelting snow as I dashed from my illegally parked car to the restaurant.

Now, safe and warm inside, I'm pelted again, this time by self-doubt. Rather than reenergize me, Andi's deflating me like a balloon.

"Oh, I think dogs *do* have personalities," she says in response to my opening gambit—a show-offy airing of my trusty "only persons can have personalities" sound byte, which usually goes over so well. "You're just getting hung up on semantics," she adds, as though excusing my folly. And of course, as soon as she says it, I realize that's exactly what I've been doing. I've been a literalist, allowing the derivation of the word to drive its meaning, when in fact it has evolved beyond its origins, so that the thing it describes—the set of reflexes, impulses, traits, and responses that differentiate one individual from all others—is absolutely something dogs possess as well. Also cats and parrots and dolphins, and for all I know geckos and crawfish and supermodels.

And I suddenly realize that that's how I've been treating Dusty all along—how I've treated all my dogs, and everyone else's too: as individuals, equals, *personalities*. While it's true that Dusty exhibits many traits I associate with his breed, when I interact with him it's not his Sheltieness that I engage with—it's his *Dusty*-ness. Competing as a team enhances my appreciation of *him* and of the role he plays as my partner and as an athlete.

Humbled, I toy with my eggplant ravioli. Andi is having a salad. How anyone can be satisfied with a bowl of chilly greens in the ferocious throes of an arctic squall is something I'll never understand. But then, Andi's salad is no mere romaine-and-bottled-dressing affair; it's arugula and maché with mandarin orange segments, extra-virgin olive oil, balsamic vinegar, and, most tantalizingly, candied walnuts. One of which I end up asking to try. It's delicious. Score another point for the distaff side.

This is one of the reasons I connected with her early on. We do seem to share some demographics. We're about the same age, both urban, both professional, and our cultural touchstones overlap. She, like me, clearly appreciates food that is actually food. She's also a bit of an agility tourist, as I was until recently. In fact the sudden increase in my competitive activity with Dusty surprised her, and she says so. I try to explain the quest for glory, but it comes out sounding cliché and self-serving, not to mention plain silly in view of the dog on which I'm banking my hopes. True, Andi is one of Dusty's biggest supporters and has always been gratifyingly observant of every corner I've turned with him. Unfortunately, it's usually in the way you'd congratulate a teenager for getting past bed-wetting. The idea of Dusty as championship material is more of a conceptual leap than I can decently ask her to make.

Still, she seems to understand that when I say "glory," what I really mean is taking my relationship with Dusty to its highest level. Maybe once upon I time I thought that might mean ribbons, medals, MACHs, but really what I'm looking for now is just a validation of something I'm perfectly capable of recognizing all by myself: harmony, sympathy, congruity—translated into movement, grace, achievement—for me and my dog.

Andi gets it. But then, her animal IQ is stratospheric. She's had dogs since childhood. When I first met her several years ago she was training a lovely, sweet-souled golden retriever named Whisper. She retired Whisper just shy of competing in excellent, due to time constraints (Andi's) and age issues (Whisper's) but has compensated by giving her a new career as a therapy dog. Whisper works with very young children with developmental disabilities, and from what Andi tells me, with great success. In addition, she does pet visits in the pediatric unit, cheering up hospitalized children. "Though the parents get as much out of her as the kids," Andi says. "Sometimes more."

One of Whisper's current patients is a twelve-year-old autistic boy who looks like he's in his late teens (he wears size-13 shoes). In just two months, he's gone from having an almost primal fear of dogs to petting and stroking Whisper—amazing progress, and a testament to Whisper's character. (What the hell, to her *personality*.)

In the meantime, Andi has taken on another, younger golden, Kelly; this despite living in a 750-square-foot apartment. "The dogs take up about a third of it," she says with a bemused shrug. "I guess I should be thankful it's not more."

This is something else she and I share; we're both on our second agility dogs. And like Dusty, Kelly isn't quite as proficient as her illustrious predecessor. She's goofier than Whisper, for one thing, and more easily distracted. She's also shamelessly flirtatious. I've been jolted to attention more than once by her large head plunging amorously into my lap. "What can I say, she's boy crazy," Andi will apologize with a sigh. "When I walk her, she'll start getting all wiggly and excited when she sees a man two blocks away. It's embarrassing." So much so that today, when I tell Andi my theory that Dusty's various pathologies are amplified reflections of my own, she snorts and says, "I wonder what Kelly's behavior says about *me*." I have to laugh as well. The idea of cool-as-spearmint Andi as some kind of slurpy man chaser is beyond ridiculous. So, is that another of my pet theories shot down?

Maybe, maybe not. Andi has an idea of how to find out for sure. She is, it turns out, a big proponent of pet psychics, or "animal communicators," as she calls them. What's more, she believes anyone can "read" an animal—it's a matter of focus, clearing the mental space for your mind to receive what the animal has to "say."

"The last time I 'talked' to Whisper," she tells me now, as I greedily eye her last few candied walnuts, "I was going to get her a new collar, and I asked her what color she wanted. And she said, clear as a bell: 'Fuchsia.' My jaw just dropped. What dog knows fuchsia? I wasn't even sure what color that was myself. Anyway, I asked a professional animal communicator about it and she said dogs pick up on all sorts of things—Whisper might have heard it on TV. I guess I do have the TV on a lot, and Whisper does seem to watch."

This is all sounding a tad dubious to me, and my initial urge is to scoff; part of me is still the jaded, urban cynic I was at the beginning of this adventure—the kind of man who sneered at the idea of giving up his weekends in pursuit of some kind of freakish organized dog jogging. But that knee-jerk reaction is quickly overwhelmed by my genuine curiosity, my respect for this woman's opinion, and, ultimately, by my vow to explore *any* technology that might work.

I've finished the last of my ravioli now and I'm still hungry. Behold the curse of being brought up Italian. Light eating is, for us, a sign of moral laxity. I'd order something else, but the lunch hour is drawing to a close. I quell my hunger and return to the subject of pet psychics—excuse me, animal communicators. "You say anyone can do this?" I ask, fighting back another flurry of skepticism. "So, me, for instance? I could do it?"

She nods matter-of-factly, as though I've asked her whether she thinks me capable of operating a doorknob. "I went to a workshop with a communicator a few years ago," she says, tossing aside a flap of corn-silk hair that's fallen over one eye. "She got me talking to a goat, who gave me a very clear picture of a Thanksgiving dinner table. I talked to his owner later, who said that as a matter of fact he *did* allow the goat in the house on Thanksgiving. Not that the owner's wife was real happy about it. The goat remembered that too."

I'm talking to an otherwise eminently sane woman about the domestic travails of a barnyard goat. Suddenly, I'm feeling quite strikingly postmillennial.

I ask about the communicator who ran this workshop. Possibly it's someone I can contact about Dusty. Andi enthusiastically endorses this. "The only problem," she says after finishing off the last walnut (damn her), "is that she's not local. I wish she'd come to Chicago and do a class. I looked into it once, but you have to get a certain number of people to sign up and pay in advance and . . ." She shrugs. "The logistics were too much for me."

"So . . . what does that mean? I'd have to get on a plane and go to *her?*" I try to imagine Dusty cooped up in the cargo hold of a jet. By the time it touched down, he'd need a hell of a lot more than an animal communicator.

Andi shakes her head. "You don't need to go anywhere. You can have a consultation over the phone."

Now my credulity really is stretched thin. "What, she 'reads' an animal over a phone line? How the hell does that work? Do I have to put Dusty on the horn? He's not much of a conversationalist, you know. Sometimes he goes for days without saying a word. You know how kids are."

She gives me a sideways "you know that's not what I mean" look and says, "No, you don't have to put Dusty 'on the horn.' You have him in the room with you, and you have a series of questions you've prepared, and the communicator reads Dusty's answers *through* you." A waiter comes to clear the table and his burly arms momentarily bisect our view, which interrupts the almost trancelike state I've fallen into. When he retreats, I feel like I've been led into la-la land, but by baby steps, so only now that I've arrived can I see how far I've come. I look over my shoulder and there's the distant shore of the realm of reason. I've abandoned the sunlit legacy of the Enlightenment for the vapors of mystic hoo-ha. "Whatever works," I repeat to myself. "Whatever the hell works." Plus, really, going back to my Italian childhood, how much difference is there between splashing my forehead with holy water to ward off the devil and Dusty having a telepathic chin wag over my land line? And finally, there's Andi sitting across from me, looking radiantly confident from beneath her untroubled brow, and who am I to mount my mewling little misgivings in opposition?

All right, then, I'll do it. Anything short of dancing naked in a pentagram. And possibly even that, if I'm asked nicely. *Whatever. Works.*

CHAPTER 24

Psyched

Swayed by Andi's impassioned testimonial, I move ahead with the idea of consulting an animal communicator. But try as I might, I can't bring myself to do it over the phone. It's taken a tremendous effort to overcome my innate skepticism to the point of entertaining the idea of "dog whispering" at all. When I try to factor in the belief that it can be done across three time zones, the whole rickety apparatus falls down around my ankles and I have to reconstruct it from scratch. I decide, for my own benefit if not Dusty's, that I need someone right here in my house, looking him square in the eye.

I go online and find a local practitioner named Rachel Tisza. Her Web site is so adorable that one look sends me into a kind of diabetic seizure, but her credentials seem solid enough, and there are lots of testimonials. "That means nothing," my inner cynic snarls from the locked cell to which I've temporarily banished him. "People are crazy." Well, yes. There is that. But some crazy people win agility titles, and I'm not nearly as picky as I used to be.

When Rachel arrives at the house, I'm surprised to find she's smaller than I anticipated—a slip of a girl, really—wearing a big fur coat and fur boots, which, she wastes no time making clear to me, are all fake. She's pretty and vivacious, and the moment she steps through the door the house seems smaller. Petite she may be, but she has *presence*.

Carmen takes to her immediately, as she usually does with visitors. Dusty is much more wary, circling her suspiciously, occasionally ducking in for a sniff, then backing away with menacing snarls.

I fetch Rachel a glass of water, and when I come back she's seated primly on the ottoman with Carmen practically climbing into her lap. "Sorry about that," I say as I order Carmen away. "It's the way she is. She's anybody's bitch."

It's a quip I've made a thousand times, but Rachel gives it so big a laugh I feel like it's the first time. Okay, that's a point in her favor. I guess I'm anybody's bitch, myself. "It's all right," she says a moment later. "We're just getting acquainted. She's been telling me how much she loves company."

"Carmen said nothing—she's a dog," retorts my inner cynic

I hold my tongue, however. Rachel is growing on me, and I'm a bit taken aback by how energetic and funny she is. This isn't the kind of earnest, gooey, New Age beginning I'd anticipated. I'm getting the feeling that, whether or not I end up believing a word this woman says, I'm in for a good show.

As I sit in the chair to Rachel's left, Dusty rounds on her with a volley of ferocious barking, as though blaming her for being seated so close to me. "Dusty, *quiet*," I snap. Then I point to the floor and say, "Down." He lowers himself to his elbows with a visible sulk.

Dusty continues to utter a low growl, just shy of being worthy of reprimand. I shrug and give Rachel my standard apology for his behavior: "Sorry, he's a rescue."

"Oh, he didn't like that!" she says. "He just shot you a look and said, '*You're* a rescue.'"

"Um . . . sorry?"

"He doesn't like you telling people he's a rescue. It embarrasses him."

Ooookay. "Anyway," I continue, "as I explained on the phone, I want to get some insight into Dusty's feelings, because I run him in agility competitions and I'm not really sure he likes it."

Rachel looks at Dusty and furrows her brow, then says, "He's telling me he likes it fine."

I look at Dusty too. He looks back but remains a closed book. I turn back to Rachel, "What in particular does he like about it?"

She pauses a moment, as if putting the question to him, then says, "He likes the validation. Well, that and spending time with you. He likes knowing he has value in your life. He's very insecure about that."

"Insecure?"

"Oh, yes. He's still not sure he . . . Hold on a moment." She looks at Carmen and then turns back to me. "Carmen says Dusty is always asking her, 'Do you think they're happy with us?'" She pauses. "Carmen says it irritates her. She's always telling Dusty, 'I have no intention of going anywhere.'"

I laugh, because that does sound like Carmen. "So, Dusty has abandonment issues?"

"Oh, yes. Neglect issues too."

"Good God! He's hardly neglected. I mean, I'm here every

day. I work from home, and . . ." I make a gesture to take in the totality of the environment.

Rachel quickly shakes her head. "Oh, I'm not talking about you. This is in his past; he suffered a lot of neglect when he was very young. He's telling me now, he—" She pauses, as if waiting for him to finish a sentence. "He says he was often ignored. They'd forget to feed him or even give him water."

"Who's 'they'?"

She grimaces and cocks her head. Dusty cocks his head right back at her. "I'm not getting a clear picture. Dusty says there were a lot of people around all the time, coming and going. But no one was central to him; no one paid much attention to him." She shifts her weight, as though preparing to deliver bad news. "I get the impression he was bred in a puppy mill."

Yikes. I'm glad Vicky Bruning's not around to hear that. This certainly explains his wonky looks. I give him a swift reappraisal; he's twisted up like a pretzel so he can scratch behind his ear—not his most flattering angle. "So . . . I don't get it. If he's been so starved for attention, why is he so standoffish? He's the least affectionate dog I've ever had. I've met cuddlier iguanas."

Another pause. "He says he shuns affection because he's convinced it won't last. He doesn't want to get too dependent on it and then lose it."

"Oh, for God's sake," I say, looking at Dusty. "Butch it up."

Rachel giggles, then says, "When you want to be physical with him, try petting his right side with your left hand. That's the best way to make sure that loving energy flows unimpeded."

I nod, jotting this down on a pad. "I can't believe you're actually taking notes," my inner cynic chimes in again.

"So," I continue, "is Dusty jealous of Carmen, then?"

"No, no," Rachel says. "He likes having her around, though he wishes she'd interact with him more. She's sort of like the classic older sister who looks down her nose at the kid brother. He—" She pauses again and looks at Carmen. "Carmen says he can be a pest. Like I said, classic sibling dynamic. But Dusty's making it very clear he wouldn't want to be an only child. In fact his exact words are, 'That would be very impossible for me.'"

Something in my chest goes twinge. Possibly I'm a sucker, but "very impossible" is exactly the sort of phrase I'd expect Dusty to use. Along with "Hey! Hey! Move along there, pal!" and "Are you gonna finish that? Well, are you?"

I clear my throat and say, "For someone who craves companionship so much, he really has no use for the other dogs in the neighborhood. He not only has no canine friends, he's actively hostile to them. I'm talking open aggression. And yet when I take him to agility class, he's as meek as a lamb." (As if on cue, the meek little lamb erupts in fury at a DHL truck passing the house.)

Rachel sighs. "Yes. Yes, I'm seeing all that now. What it amounts to is that when you're walking with him and other dogs approach you, he can sense their social energy, and it makes him nervous and unsure of himself. He doesn't know what it is or how to respond, so he gets aggressive. But in agility class, the dogs are otherwise occupied, so he can ignore them and relax."

"He's not so much relaxed as comatose."

"Oh, by 'relax' I just mean he doesn't have to be 'on.' And he's not comatose, he's observing. He feels more comfortable watching others than engaging with them."

"Exactly like you," notes my inner cynic, who's suddenly not so cynical.

"He's that way with other people too," I say. "He shies away from them, won't have anything to do with them."

Rachel shrugs. "He's just not interested in other people. He's only interested in you."

"Well, what can I do to get him over that?"

She gives me a penetrating look. "Why would you want to?"

I sputter for a moment. I don't really have an answer. "Well," I say, grasping, "it'd be nice, for instance, when we have people over, if he weren't so antisocial. When we're having a dinner party or something—I mean, I'm usually the one who's cooking, plus, you know, I've got guests to entertain, and it's just . . . well, having to keep an eye on Dusty too, that's just one more burden on my shoulders."

Rachel looks at Dusty for a while and then looks at me even longer. I'm beginning to squirm beneath her gaze when she says, "Dusty tells me you like that."

I blink. "He tells you *what?*"

"He's having a hard time expressing himself," she says. "But what I'm getting from him is that you *like* keeping track of him during parties." She gives him a quick glance, as if to confirm this. "He says you get nervous with a bunch of people around, unless you have a job. That's why you like to do the cooking and keep tabs on him. It makes you feel less awkward when you have something to do."

I can feel my face flush. It's almost as if I've been physically struck. I can't argue with any of this. In fact, hearing it spoken, I know it's undeniably true. I *do* feel at sea among people—even good friends in my own home. There's something about the form-less drift of casual cocktail chatter that unnerves and unmans me. I need touchstones; I need anchors.

Goddamn it. What the hell is happening? Who exactly is being "whispered" here?

"It sounds like you and Dusty both like structure," Rachel con-tinues. "That's why agility is so good for you both."

It's a moment before I can speak, my throat still constricted by emotion. But I'm grateful for the chance to get back to the origi-nal issue. "So," I ask, trying to disguise the tremor that's crept into my voice, "what can I do to give him more confidence when we're competing?"

She recommends aromatherapy and a few herbal extracts, and I take up my pen again to scribble down the names she rattles off. "Before we wrap things up," I say, "I was wondering if you could give Dusty a body scan." Andi had suggested this—said it could be very enlightening, especially for animals whose backgrounds are unknown.

"Sure!" Rachel says, as though I've requested the most unex-ceptional thing in the world. I might've just asked her to lend me a fiver or sing a few bars of "Eleanor Rigby." She puts her hands on her knees and looks hard at Dusty. After a few moments, she says, "Well, this is interesting."

"What?"

"It seems Dusty is nearsighted."

"You're kidding. Nearsighted?"

"Yes. He's telling me so now. When he's with you in the agility ring, it's like the obstacles come up out of nowhere, which makes him kind of timid. He sticks by you, doesn't he?"

"Yes. Most of the time, anyway."

"That's why. He doesn't want to get too far away from you because running toward things he can't see makes him a little hesitant."

"Well, I do *tell* him what's coming up. He's just got to listen to me." "You're whining," says my inner cynic, who seems now to have changed sides.

"He does listen to you. And he's trying to get better at it. But be patient with him."

I sit back, trying to absorb this.

"Anything else I can help you with?" she asks.

I shake my head. "I think this is about all I can take for one day."

She laughs, then in a great cheery bustle she's on her feet and out the door, once more back in a world that now seems far too small for her.

It's minutes before my heart stops pounding.

I look at Dusty—who seems entirely unperturbed—and say, "Geez, boy. Way to knock the old man on his ass."

Then I go and give him a big hug.

And what do you know, he lets me.

CHAPTER 25

On, Blitzen!

With my fresh new outlook, we reenter the world of competitive canine agility at the biggest trial of the year: Blitzen Agility Club's, held at the McCormick Place convention center on Chicago's lakefront. The event is cosponsored by the International Kennel Club, and the event is known in the agility world as IKC.

It's also much more than an agility trial; it's part of a self-described "cluster" of dog shows, including obedience and conformation trials (Westminster-style "best of breed" shows), plus vendors of every kind of dog-related product you can imagine and a few you probably can't. As Dusty and I wind our way through the bazaar-like environs, we pass booths selling T-shirts, pot holders, paperweights, frames, porcelain figurines, decals, canned food, dry food, vitamins, snack treats, mouse pads, tea towels, shampoos, brushes, clippers, shears, leashes, collars, clothing, furniture, photo portraits, oil portraits, caricatures, bowls and dishes, welcome mats, baseball caps, cutting boards, crates, blankets, mats, purses, luggage, plush toys, squeaky toys, pull toys, flower pots,

cookie jars, temporary tattoos, pooper scoopers, pet-stain sol-
vents, books, videos, and magazines. The Anti-Cruelty Society
has a booth, as do several rescue societies, so you can just bypass
the accessories and get yourself an actual dog.

All of this takes place in a hall the size of an airplane hangar, so
that Dusty and I get turned around and have to retrace our steps
more than once in our quest for the agility rings. Dusty's stress
level visibly rises as my own frustration mounts, so that at one
point I pull him over to a comparatively isolated spot between
two concrete posts and give him a hit of two herbal remedies Rachel Tisza recommended. One is supposed to boost confidence
and self-esteem, the other instill courage and focus. I'd intended
to use them just before our runs, but clearly he needs them right
now. I look left, then right, making sure the coast is clear, then
take a couple of hits myself. I'm feeling a bit sheepish after taking
so much time off, worried about whether team All Fours will immediately welcome me back into its midst.

Finally, we stumble across agility, which is tucked into an al-
cove off the main hall. The adjacent crating space is relatively
small, but the All Fours crew has, as usual, arrived early and staked
its claim. There's room enough here for everybody—and almost
everybody will be here at some point over the weekend. This year
marks a return to IKC for the All Fours crew after a boycott due
to a variety of objections ranging from the inferiority of the flooring to obstructions on the courses. This year isn't without its of-
fenses, however—the organizers seem to have neglected to
designate a crating area; competitors were left to just pick a spot
at random—which explains why we're all butted up against the
standard poodle grooming station. The constant roar of blow-

dryers is nerve-shredding but does provide some comic relief—a canine edition of *America's Next Top Model*. The shaving and snipping and sculpting are fast, furious, and constant, despite which the finished dogs look remarkably like a kindergarten art project involving cotton balls, drinking straws, and paste. And the bits of white fur flying everywhere give me a belated yuletide feeling.

Fortunately, all the grumbling and the chaos allow me to slip into the All Fours midst unnoticed—and thus unchided for my long absence. Despite the general kvetching about the facility, there's a certain buoyancy in the air. It must be because of the social factor; nearly everyone's come out for the event: Andi, Jason, Gus and Deb, and on down the roll call. Dee is here too, but only as a fleeting presence; she's not running Kaleigh in agility, choosing instead to enter Kaleigh's offspring Payton in conformation. It's strange to see Dee in lipstick and wearing her styling smock. She looks like a different woman—a TV-movie version of herself. The trademark ponytail is still in place, however, and the way she's bustling about this morning you'd better stay out of its way. If she turns swiftly on her heel, it could crack like a whip and take your eye out.

I've brought along my own trademark: fresh cinnamon rolls from the famous Ann Sather restaurant on Chicago's North Side. I don't know how it happened that this particular delicacy has become expected of me at these big events; I only know I don't dare show up without it—especially today, since the gooey goodness might be just the thing to help me seduce my way back into the All Fours ranks.

As it happens, I've been so focused on the rolls that I've neglected to bring something much more fundamental: running shoes.

I'm here in my big black winter boots, with nothing to change into. That means I'll have to go clomping around the ring like L'il Abner.

My standard and jumpers runs are literally back-to-back, my walk-throughs for both taking place simultaneously. I end up racing back and forth between the rings, like a sitcom character who's wining and dining two different dates in two adjacent restaurants.

Of course all this rushing around and nervous energy is fatal for the actual runs. Dusty takes one look at me and visibly cringes; I must be radioactive with anxiety. In our standard run, he gives all the obstacles so wide a berth that you might suspect them of being electrified. In jumpers he manages a fair number of jumps—I'll give him that. Some of them are even the right ones.

The two successive flops leave me crestfallen, but my competitive spirit is restored watching Jason run his Airedale, Pebbles, in the standard ring. Pebbles is usually an energetic competitor, but despite Jason's exhortations she's distracted today, dragging her heels, sniffing around the floor.

I suddenly realize what's about to happen and mutter "uh-oh." A moment later Pebbles drops into a squat and Jason throws his hands in the air in exasperation. I feel bad for him but am somewhat relieved that my run won't be the day's most disastrous.

I hurry off to give Dusty the news. I zip open his crate and peer in at him. He blinks up at me as though I've interrupted him midsnooze. "Hey, boy," I say, "guess what? Pebbles just beshat the standard course." He doesn't seem quite as amused as I'd hoped, and I realize he's had a rough morning—beginning with parking in the remote lot and having to take a shuttle bus here to the building. It was his first experience with public transportation, and he was aghast at all the people, dogs, and equipment jammed in on all sides of him. He even consented to sit in my lap, a sign of real distress. Making matters worse, two women in the seat in front of us kept reaching back to pet him, despite my repeated requests that they refrain from touching my dog. Apparently, the roar of the engine garbled my speech, and when I said, "He's very shy; he doesn't like people," they heard, "Please drape your meaty fingers all over my pet."

From the shuttle he was hurled directly into back-to-back standard and jumpers runs with a gasping, manic handler. It's no wonder he's shut down. So much for my commitment to considering Dusty's needs first, to making agility positive and constructive for him. It'd take more than a whiff of herbal courage to counteract the kind of stress I put him through this morning. Unfortunately, I don't have ready access to Xanax.

My sole attempt at removing him from his crate is a bust. Just as he sticks his head out and tentatively surveys the scene, one of the poodles decides it doesn't actually *like* being made up like a fifteen-dollar dessert and begins loudly protesting. Dusty draws back like Punxsutawney Phil from a volley of flashbulbs.

He's only slightly less unnerved when the FAST class finally rolls around at the very end of the day. I take him to the practice jump just outside the ring and lead him over it a dozen times. He's distracted and unresponsive at first, but by the time we finish he's gliding over it like an antelope. I have a good feeling about this run. I've sketched out a course that highlights Dusty's strengths and avoids his weaknesses (read: the teeter), and takes into consideration that he's significantly slower that some of his opponents. I'm keeping it real, thinking about what Dusty can do (and do happily), rather than focusing on the ribbon I'm dying to win.

Dee's approval of my charted course (she even high-fives me!) leaves me brimming with confidence as I approach the line. It's been a very long day, and there's part of me that's bone weary. But I won't give into it till we're on the other side of this run. Dusty looks relaxed and ready—we're all set up for magic to happen.

But when the run starts, he won't come anywhere near me. I can't understand what the problem is. Then I start to feel the fatigue in my legs and realize: the boots. I make a sweeping gesture and call out, "Dusty, chute!" meanwhile *stomp, stomp, stomping* toward the obstacle in question. Dusty quickly decides his best option lies in the opposite direction and skitters off to another obstacle. Understandable, I suppose. If I had limbs like breadsticks I doubt very much I'd want to get in the way of a pair of steel-toed monstrosities with soles thick enough to break my spine in one salsa move.

We finish the course only in the sense that we clear the finish jump. Everything else about the run has been a noisy, messy failure. Looking over my shoulder, I can see two separate places on the course where my boots piled up the cheap flooring behind me. I've only just returned to competition, and I'm already making an enemy of the handler who's going to have to run the course after me.

This is all particularly embarrassing because a number of All Fours people have stayed all this time to watch me run. They've stood on the sidelines as virtually the entire hall emptied out, waiting patiently to see Dusty and me dissolve into quivering bits of hair and teeth. They're all very nice about it, and each of them finds something encouraging to say about the run, though the only unarguably nice thing about it is that it's over and we can all go home.

I leash Dusty, don my coat, and head outside just as a shuttle pulls away for the parking lot. Well, never mind, I'll be first in line for the next one.

Except, there *is* no line. People don't file in behind me; they swarm up to where I'm standing till we're about seven abreast. This is very annoying. More arrivals keep crowding in from behind till we have a certifiable throng here, all awaiting the next bus.

Eventually, the shuttle wheels into view and putters up to where we're standing. And what do you know, it stops right in front of me. "First bit of luck I've had all day," I think, and when the door opens with a hiss, I step up into the empty vehicle—and Dusty starts pulling back. He remembers this contraption from this morning, and there's no way he's getting back on it voluntarily. "Come on, boy," I say, tugging him as the crowd closes in behind us.

But he won't budge. And the harder I tug, the more determinedly he resists, till all of a sudden I find myself dangling an empty collar at the end of the leash, and people are crying, "Loose dog! Loose dog!"

I dismount the step and try to fight my way through the horde of people pushing to get on the shuttle. It's like climbing uphill against an avalanche. Meantime the shouts of "Loose dog!" are coming from farther and farther up the ramp.

Finally, I succeed in bursting through the wall of humanity, just in time to see Dusty skittering toward the door leading back into the building. "Dusty, *no!*" I declaim with the paralyzing intonations of the Old Testament God, and he accordingly stops in place as though I've turned him into a pillar of salt. I clamber over to him, reattach his collar, then pluck him up like a melon and hold him tight in my arms. I don't care if he hates it.

I turn around in time to see the shuttle door close and the shuttle itself lumber away, laden with passengers. There are now about two dozen other people awaiting the next one, and I'm behind all of them. The sky is darkening and so is my mood. I feel unspeakable, and so don't speak.

Dusty of course doesn't either. Even if he could, he wouldn't dare.

CHAPTER 26

Rescue Me

My decision to return to agility suddenly seems hasty and sentimental. I'm so frustrated that I actually debate whether to go back for the second day of competition. But in the morning everything seems slightly more hopeful, as it often does.

When I return to McCormick Place, I drive past the remote lot and instead park in the garage attached to the building. It's more expensive, but you can walk from your car directly into the IKC hall. No more hazarding the dreaded shuttle. Also no more need for boots. I can wear my running shoes in the car, eliminating any chance that I'll forget to bring them.

It's a good thing I've avoided traumatizing Dusty with the shuttle because our morning is just as jam-packed as yesterday. Once again our first two runs of the day occur almost simultaneously, but I decide to breeze through jumpers and save my energy and focus for the standard run. We have yet to qualify in standard, and I'm eager to make that breakthrough.

As it turns out, the run is like a Bizarro World version of every other standard run we've ever done. Dusty refuses every obstacle *except* the teeter, which he tosses off like he does it every day and twice before breakfast. Everything else—no go. He won't do the A-frame, won't attempt the dogwalk, refuses even to sit on the table. He stands atop it staring at me while I go crimson shouting, "Sit! Sit!" and hunch ever lower, thrusting my palm downward. The expression on his face is one of expectant bemusement, like this is all the setup to a burlesque-style pratfall and why don't I just get to it already? Eventually, we're whistled off the course, which is about the most embarrassing thing that can happen out there that doesn't involve bodily fluids.

Quite a few of my colleagues have watched all this unfold, and I'm too mortified now to accompany them back to the crating area, so I just give them a wave as I stride past.

"Where are you going?" Andi asks.

"Sheltie rescue booth," I reply, gesturing toward Dusty. "I need to return this."

In the hours I have to kill before my FAST run I decide, in true neurotic fashion, that by now some exhibitors may have left the show, enabling me to move my car closer to the elevator. I check on Dusty, who's contentedly snuggled in his crate—"Be right back, boy," I tell him—then I leave the hall and head back to the garage.

As it happens, there are indeed a few open spaces nearer the elevator. I puff up with pride at my cleverness. Never mind that the thirty seconds I'll save at the end of the day are more than canceled out by the ten minutes this mission will cost me. Who's keeping track?

I get in the car, start the ignition, back out of my space, and head toward the elevator bank. I've gone about twenty feet when something under the hood goes *whunk* and the whole car shakes like it's sneezed. There's a horrible, acrid smell, and my dashboard lights up in red.

I'm reasonably certain none of this augurs well, so I pull into the nearest open stall, turn off the engine, and consult my owner's manual. A bit of index scanning and page flipping lead me to the conclusion that the drive belt has snapped.

All right. These things happen. I'm a grown man, I can handle it. I get out of the car and head down to the garage office to arrange a tow. Turns out they don't offer this service themselves but very helpfully provide the numbers of nearby companies who do.

Alas, it seems the garage's eight-foot ceiling rules out the aid of every single tow truck in metropolitan Chicago. When I get to the point at which I'm actually verbally abusing one of the operators—"You mean to tell me you've *never* been asked to tow a car from a parking garage before? This is the *first time ever* in your history? Buddy, you are a freakin' *liar*"—that I realize I am perhaps setting up a major karma backlash and should maybe just hang up, take a deep breath, and reassess the situation.

All the towing companies have told me that I have to get the car out of the garage before they can help me. The owner's manual, however, emphatically says not to operate the car with the drive belt broken. But it should only take about ninety seconds of downhill coasting to get the car onto the street. It seems like my only available option.

I go back to the car, start it up again, and pull out of the parking stall. I promptly discover that in the intervening half hour the steering has frozen. I can only manage to turn the wheel with truly Herculean effort. Part of me is glad to know that all those years at the gym, building my upper-body strength, are finally paying off, but mostly I'm just really, really annoyed.

I maneuver the car down the exit ramps; it's like steering the *Queen Mary* through gravel. I need both hands and tremendous focus, and I find it helps to unleash a steady stream of the most offensive expletives in the lexicon. Terms I didn't even know I knew.

It takes a good six minutes, but finally the exit is before me and I cautiously roll out onto the street. As if anything could be easy in this debacle, I immediately realize that I can't just leave my car on the busy thoroughfare; cars are whipping by at forty, fifty miles per hour, and there is no parking lane. Everything is traffic, traffic, traffic. I have to keep driving till I find someplace I can safely stow my lemon.

This takes an agonizingly long time, and leads me farther and farther away from the convention center into increasingly dicey neighborhoods. Eventually, I find a handicapped space on a small industrial side street. Well, my car is handicapped, no?

It takes several minutes to pull into it, because by this point the steering wheel might as well be set in cement. When I finally have it in place and remove my hands, my arms feel like overcooked pappardelle noodles.

I call the last towing service I spoke with and arrange for them to come collect the car and take it to a service center. When I tell them I can't wait with the vehicle, they ask me to leave the doors unlocked and the keys on the mat, which I don't mind doing. Theft would be welcome at this point.

After glancing at my watch, I turn and scurry back to the trial; my FAST run is quickly approaching and my parking greediness has eaten up much more time than I thought. As I trot the several blocks to the exhibition hall, I'm mindful to sidestep patches of ice and snow, because of course today I'm cleverly wearing running shoes to tromp around outdoors while yesterday I sported snow boots for indoor athletics.

Winded, I plunk into my chair and wait for everyone to ask, "Where have you been?" But of course no one does, because why would they assume I've been anywhere? It's a sad moment when you've been tossed out in the world to deal with a dramatic personal crisis, over which you eventually and with difficulty triumph, only to return and discover no one's even noticed you were gone.

Now stranded, I call Jeffrey to come and rescue me. He shows up just before my FAST run and proceeds to charm all my colleagues. Dusty even allows him to hold him in his lap. I sense the makings of an insurrection. Fortunately, this is averted by the run itself—though perhaps "fortunately" isn't the word. I might rather have had Jeffrey's easy amiability push me off into the shadows than to be the focus of attention when so much is going wrong. Dusty, perhaps lulled by Jeffrey's special-guest-star aura, treats the course like a cakewalk. He has all the urgency of a summer breeze. And at the send bonus he totally falls apart. I know he's nearsighted, and I know it's five feet away—but it's a tunnel, for God's sake. Usually, he can't resist a tunnel opening. I shouldn't be able to *hold him back* from a tunnel opening. But today he avoids it like it's one of al Qaeda's cavern redoubts.

Jeffrey, obviously concerned lest this calamity be lost to history, records the whole thing on his digital camera. "Want to see the replay?" he asks when I rejoin him.

"I'd rather go blind," I reply.

Much to my chagrin, Jeffrey's parked in the lot, meaning we'll have to brave the blasted shuttle again.

"We don't need to take it," he says. "We can walk." Despite my battle with the car, my trek through the snow, and my embarrassing run, he's serious. Fine. It's a nice night; a little fresh air won't hurt.

We leave by way of several flights of escalator (you can imagine Dusty's reaction to an actual moving piece of machinery. Needless to say, I carry him) and exit onto the street, where the air is indeed very sweet and soothing and the roar of traffic about half what it was this afternoon. Dusty trots contentedly behind us as we make our way around the corner. Timidly, Jeffrey broaches the elephant in the room: "I'm sorry your day was such a disaster. You probably regret going back, huh?"

"You'd think so," I say. Yet strangely, as I reflect on the whole calamitous weekend, what shines through most clearly are the people. Dee's irrepressible spirit, the glow on Deb's face when she Q'd with Brittany, even the smile on Jason's baby girl, who showed up today and who was clearly over the moon at being surrounded by so many fluffy pals. "Actually, I kind of enjoyed it. It was a good day. A really *good day*." And suddenly I realize that my last calamitous day—the one that drove me to quit agility altogether—occurred at a trial I attended alone, without any of my colleagues.

While I consider the significance of this, Jeffrey and I lapse into a short silence, walking along absorbed in our own thoughts. When we finally look up and survey our surroundings, we realize we've somehow ended up along a stretch of underground loading docks, surrounded by still, dark trucks the size of single-family houses. There's not another human being anywhere in sight.

Jeffrey looks over his shoulder. "We might've taken a wrong turn," he says with admirable aplomb.

"Ya think?" I add, rather unhelpfully.

"Should we try to retrace our steps?"

I look behind us: loading docks, as far as the eye can see. "I don't know. Maybe we'd be better off finding some stairs back up to ground level."

And so we tramp on, Dusty valiantly bringing up the rear, for what seems to be a very long time; all conversation has now died, quashed by the weight of our growing apprehension. It's getting dimmer and dimmer down here, the only illumination coming from oily orange lamps over the top of each loading ramp. Our shadows dance wildly around us. I try to whistle to keep our spirits up, but the only tune I can think of is the theme from *Touch of Evil*, which seems inauspicious.

At one point we come across a big chain-link fence, padlocked and topped with razor wire. Looking through it, we can see the parking lot, tantalizingly close. "If we could just get by," Jeffrey says, giving the gate a good rattle.

I bend down to examine its lower edge. "There's a gap," I say.

"We can probably squeeze underneath. We're both thin." But Jeffrey has worn his best cowboy boots, jeans, and jacket, and I know better than to ask him even to consider the idea of scrabbling in the dirt under a length of snarly fence. Because of course cowboys aren't ever meant to get dirty.

So we continue. After what feels like ages, we find the flight of stairs we've been hoping for and collectively let out a big sigh; it seems we've both been holding our breath. We scamper up to ground level again and find ourselves behind one of the main buildings—a forbidding wall of concrete. We're almost thrown back into despondency, but a nearby fire door that's been propped open provides the light at the end of our tunnel. "We're in, we're in!" I cry, and Jeffrey quickly joins me as I yank it wide open.

Light spills out, and music.

And suddenly there are people looking out at us.

A lot of people.

Natty black men in suits and bow ties, and women in brown scarves and ankle-length skirts.

"Through here," Jeffrey says, and he starts to enter.

"*Wait*, for God's sake," I say, grabbing his arm. "We can't go in there—it's a Nation of Islam convention!"

He shrugs. "So?"

"So, Muslims hate dogs! They think they're unclean. And frankly," I add, gesturing at Dusty, whose feet are now black with grime, "in this case they've got a point."

"Oh, he's little. They won't even see him."

And so he strides on in—my Jeffrey, possibly the whitest man in the universe, all done up in his Marlboro Man gear, confidently making his way among the ranks of the Farrakhan faithful, and within seconds I'm following him, trailing an actual live creature into their religious gathering. But what else can I do? It's our only way to freedom.

"Should I ask where the bar is?" Jeffrey asks over his shoulder.

Oh, yeah, he's a real smart-ass.

But a moment later he's found the mezzanine, so he gets a pass.

CHAPTER 27

Punc'd

In the wake of our across-the-board wipeout at IKC, it seems clear that aromatherapy and the essential oils with which I've been treating Dusty haven't been sufficient to calm, focus, embolden, or energize him. And to be frank, I'm starting to gag on the scent of lavender. But we've got another trial coming up, and I've been wondering what I can possibly do differently. I've already broken the bank on oils and psychics, so I decide to take a more direct approach and enlist the help of a local pet acupuncturist. Andi recommended a veterinarian who cofounded an outfit on the North Side of Chicago devoted to pet rehabilitation and hydrotherapy. "Anything that works," I remind myself. During a brief telephone consultation, I fill her in on Dusty's performance-related issues and we make an appointment.

I turn to Dusty, who's curled up on the couch, and say, "Hey, boy! How'd you like to get stabbed repeatedly and systematically by a complete stranger in a lab coat?" His ears twitch as he appears to consider it. I'll take that as a yes.

A few days later, we find ourselves checking in at the center's reception desk. The space is wide open with big, sparkling aluminum pipes running across the ceiling, and the whole place feels more like a Manhattan art gallery or an LA recording studio than a doctor's office. And it's in Lincoln Park, where real estate is worth more than the GNP of some small countries. And it's for *pets*. I find myself wondering how on earth they pay their rent. I suppose I'll have a clue once I see what they charge for the privilege of turning my dog into a voodoo doll.

We're led down a very long corridor; Dusty trots behind me on high alert. Everything in this place is so burnished and crisp that I can't help noticing how grubby my boy looks by comparison. In this particular environment, he looks like something they might sweep up in a dustpan.

We come upon a large, open therapy room, one entire side comprising a bank of windows. It's bright and cheerful, and despite the profusion of equipment—treadmills, medicine balls, trampolines, and so on—it gives an impression of aristocratic spareness. In one corner a Siberian husky is being massaged by a thin girl in flip-flops. He's lying on his side and is so completely at his ease that he casts just one ice blue glance our way as we pass, then dreamily shuts his eyes again. Meanwhile, what I presume is an arthritic black Lab is dog-paddling in a small pool, held partially aloft by a fetching yellow life jacket. Alongside him, a chipper young physical therapist guides a Newfoundland through a device that's kind of like a horizontal ladder, a doggie version of football's high-knees drills.

Dr. Cale, a gentle, curly haired presence whose smile puts us immediately at ease (well, me, anyway; Dusty is reserving judgment) joins us in the consultation room. She does exactly the right thing by ignoring him completely, thereby granting him the time and space to creep forward, check her out, and grant her his tentative approval. Though when she does finally cast a quick glance at him, he immediately recoils.

"Dusty doesn't have any health issues," I tell her. "We're here because he's got some behavioral glitches that I haven't been able to work through. He's an athlete, see," and here I feel a little charge. I love saying this about him. "He competes in canine agility, and he's very fast and very smart, but he doesn't have tremendous confidence. He's easily rattled by crowds, by noises, by the pressure, anything really. He stresses out and sort of shuts down on me. And the paradox is, at home, on his own turf, he has just the opposite problem: he's too 'on,' too aggressive—I have to rein him in to keep him from going on the attack. It's like he feels he's got to police the whole neighborhood himself. What I'm looking for is some way of balancing him out a little—take some of the aggression he exhibits at home, that take-charge drive that he has, and get him to feel it in the agility ring. And in turn take some of the reticence and caution he feels there, and bring it into play in his regular daily life." Dr. Cale looks at me with widened eyes, and I realize that I've just slapped her with a whole lot to chew on. Oh God, I'm a helicopter parent. But I can't seem to stop. "Acupuncture," I tell her. "I was hoping a little acupuncture might even him out. Anyway, we've got an agility trial the day after tomorrow and I thought it couldn't hurt."

She nods, arches an eyebrow, and makes a few notes on her chart, then says, "Well, I think you've got the right idea. But I have to tell you, acupuncture isn't something that works immediately. There may be some initial benefit for a few hours, or even a day, after the initial session, but you only obtain substantive, permanent results through ongoing treatment."

I'm crestfallen. Because, first, why does everything have to be so freakin' complicated? And also because I ought to know by now that everything *is* so freakin' complicated. I feel a little stupid, marching into this professional facility and asking for a quick fix to my dog's very character—like taking my car to a body shop and asking for a new coat of paint—blue, please, and do I have time to grab lunch while you're at it? Clearly, my conversation with Andi didn't sufficiently teach me that Dusty is Dusty, limited by both his Sheltieness and his own disposition. A quick fix can't change who he is.

"We can treat Dusty today, if you like," she says. "I just want to manage your expectations. After a single session you're unlikely to see much in the way of verifiable improvement. But if you think this is something you'd like to pursue, certainly we can start right away."

I lift Dusty onto the metal examining table. He seems to shrink, shedding mass in defiance of every known law of physics. It's my turn to shrink when Dr. Cale produces several tiny needles with purple plastic grips. They're the equivalent of the pins you'd use to attach notices to corkboard, and for a moment I envision flyers tacked to Dusty's rump: "'87 Buick Skylark, Great Condition, Best Offer." My mind is really running amok here. I'm clearly more nervous than my dog is.

The first needles go in. Dr. Cale is aligning them with what she calls Dusty's meridian lines. She sticks one on each hip; his shank does a little involuntary flinch at the first one, but after that he's fine. A good thing, because the way he's positioned he'd only have to flick his head up to tear my throat out. I massage his cheeks and tell him what a good boy he's being, and he presses his head against my chest, as though trying to seek refuge in my rib cage.

The next needles go into his forelegs; then one at the base of his skull; and after that I lose track. There are about nine in all. He looks like something from a Clive Barker horror film: *Hound of Hellraiser.*

"How long?" I ask, still stroking him.

"Ten minutes," she replies, and I hold Dusty's ruff, keeping him still, keeping him calm; he doesn't move, doesn't at all resist, so that I can't help thinking, "It's working already," despite what Dr. Cale just told me.

The top of his head is still pressed into my sternum, and I can feel his warmth seeping into me. I'll have a red mark here, no doubt, when I take my shirt off. But I like the feeling. Physical closeness of this kind isn't something I often experience with him. And it isn't just the novelty of holding my dog this way, it's also what it implies, which is trust. He's at ease, taking comfort in my proximity, finding security in my arms. The exchange is almost palpable; so much so that I begin to feel flush, dizzy. It's as though I'm the one undergoing treatment here. Dr. Cale's voice grows faint, and my vision goes all white and cottony. I'm not entirely sure what's happening.

I lift Dusty's chin so that his eyes meet mine. "Hey, buddy," I say softly, "is this some mystic woo-woo, or what?"

He stares at me a moment longer—I feel myself swirling into his eyes, like water down a bathtub drain—and realize I'm on the brink of something embarrassing, like my knees giving out or wetting myself.

Then suddenly he shakes and little purple needles go flying off in all directions, like a porcupine shedding quills. "Whoa!" I shout, half laughing, but I can already feel the air around me cool. The weird symbiotic spell has been broken, its momentary hold snapped clean.

Truth be told, I'm no longer certain we need to come back. Agility builds a strong rapport between handler and dog, but till now I had no idea *how* strong. I realize that my recent excursions into "alternative pet care" have made me far less skeptical of people like Andi communicating with their animals, and I can better understand how Carl and Kim are able to live at such close quarters with their Porties without running stark mad. It's about finding a connection with your pet—in whatever form works for both of you.

And Dusty and I *have* found what works for us. Believe me, it's *not* sharing 750 square feet—we're independent spirits, and I can't see us relishing too much intimacy. I respect his space, he respects mine; we show affection, not by cuddling and hugging, but by standing shoulder to shoulder in competition (well, shoulder to shin).

The treatment today confirmed that I *am* keenly keyed into this little critter; it strikes me as though our physical contact during the acupuncture managed to tap into not only Dusty's meridian lines but my own. Frankly, it was a tad too Vulcan mind meld for comfort—I'm not looking literally to be one with Dusty—no need to wind up scratching my ear with my foot or yapping out car windows.

Then again, maybe that wouldn't be too awful. If we did establish that kind of weird symbiotic relationship, I could just run the goddamn teeter myself.

CHAPTER 28

Not So FAST

We arrive at the Crystal Lake Regional Sports Center, the site of our very first trial, now so many months past. That was a warm day, almost torpid. I remember sweating as I toted my chair and crate into the complex. Today the whole landscape is covered with snow, and as I pull up the drive the ice cracks beneath my wheels.

And that's not the only thing that's changed. Back then Dusty entered these doors as a complete tyro. Now he's a seasoned competitor with a title to his name—Dusty NAJ. I've been on a real roller coaster lately, bouts of frustration alternating with bursts of enthusiasm—hell, I've even quit and come back again——but standing here now I can't help putting it all into perspective. We haven't come as far as I'd planned. In fact I'm embarrassed I ever thought I'd be on my way to the upper echelons of the sport by this point. But given Dusty's manifold peculiarities, it's vastly to my—to *our*—credit that we've come even as far as we have. And if we aren't exactly champions, at least I now realize what a champion *is*—and it isn't always the handler or the dog that scores the highest or wins the most ribbons.

All this is beginning to sound oddly valedictory, so I shake it out of my head. I'm in no way giving up. I still intend to see how far we can go, and I'm not convinced a novice jumpers title is anywhere near our upper limit. It's just a matter of focus, firmness, consistency, and hard work. IKC was very distracting; our reentry to competition should not have been in that three-ring circus. This event is much smaller, quieter, *tamer*. Funny, the first time we entered these doors, the din had seemed insupportable, even maddening. Now it's almost soothing: white noise, like the purr of a humidifier. Also Dusty's no longer the twitching, cringing creature he was back then. After competing in every kind of brutal condition—not to mention being subjected to aromatherapy, acupuncture, and even dog whispering—he's more thoroughly prepped than he's ever been. He's still just a scrawny little twist of pipe cleaner, but he's picked up a truckload of experience. If the way to victory isn't clear now, I don't know when it will be.

I've arrived early so I've got some time to wander. Some All Fours colleagues direct me to the Liver Lady, a small-scale entrepreneur with a table in the tiny vendors' corner. She's a bustling little woman in an apron, who's selling a variety of dog treats she cooked in her very own oven. There are samples set out on plates, and each has the kind of aroma that forces me to ask, "These are for dogs, right?" She assures me they are—also that they are *very*, *very* fresh, made with the freshest ingredients, so when I get home I better put them right in the refrigerator or she won't answer for what happens to them.

I settle on a bag of whitefish-and-potato biscuits, pay her five bucks, and move on. When I'm just far enough to be out of sight, I can't help myself: I open the bag and sample one. It's very savory, not as seasoned as I'd like, but I could easily fix that at home. I begin to wonder how many of these are actually going to end up being consumed by their target market. In my house it's going to be touch and go.

At our open jumpers walk-through, the competitors meet with our judge—one Sue Freigen, a trim, curly blond.

"I've just been on the East Coast," she says, "where there's been a nasty trend under way of handlers downing their dogs when they make a mistake, and then walking them off the course. This is intended to be punitive, and in my opinion it's harmful to the rapport between the handler and the dog. I don't want to see that kind of thing spread here. Keep in mind that your dogs don't have to do this for you. They don't have to be here. Some of them love it, sure, but all of them are doing it to please you. So stay happy, stay upbeat, and keep your dog happy too. Just remember: it doesn't matter if he gets a first-place ribbon or if he has two lines of marks on his scribe sheet—whatever happens, you're going home with the world's best dog."

It's one of the best briefing speeches I've heard—and a particularly apt message for me today, even though I'd already set my mind on keeping my cool and not allowing blunders and foul-ups to sour my mood. Given the way Dusty's been performing lately, I can use all the reinforcement I can get.

As it happens, Dusty turns in a perfectly respectable run, his best ever in this class; there are just two refusals—one too many for open. So we don't qualify, but it's a near thing. In novice it would've been a perfect score. I give Dusty a manly back rub and tell him how pleased I am. "Just keep it up, boy. I mean—no pressure, or anything. But that was *great*."

Our standard run goes better than usual too. So well that I think, "If I can just get him over the teeter we'll be home free." And a diabolical little gambit occurs to me in midrun, so that when we're making our approach I shout, "Walk it!" which is my command for the dog walk. The way I figure, if Dusty's really nearsighted, he won't notice the difference till he's halfway across, and maybe sheer momentum will keep him going after that.

But I should know better than to underestimate the little guy; he sails off the teeter like a swallow from a Capistrano rooftop.

All right, then. No Q in standard either. We finish the run to polite applause, and I feel the initial pricklings of irritation along my hairline. I close my eyes and remind myself, "No matter what happens, I'm going home with the world's best dog." When I open my eyes again, the world's best dog has his snout stuck up the anus of an affronted looking Braque du Bourbonnais.

All that's left now is our FAST run, and this is the one I've been waiting for. I've got a good feeling about it. Dusty's been running well all day, I've plotted out a plan of attack that emphasizes all his strengths, and the send bonus is a simple pair of jumps well within his comfort zone. If I can just get up enough speed, he'll be over them before he knows it. Everything is aligned to make this a qualifying run, our first in a very long time.

Finally, our moment comes. The dog before us finishes and I lead Dusty out to the line. "This is it, boy," I tell him. "Make me proud. We're going home winners tonight!" I remove his leash and collar, toss them behind me, then turn expectantly to the timekeeper.

"Go when ready," he says.

"All right, boy," I say. "Over!" And I propel myself forward, leading him toward the first jump. He follows—he clears it beautifully.

And the whistle blows.

I stop in my tracks; I can't believe it.

"Thank you," the judge says. "Run concluded."

"*What?*" I say. "But . . . why?"

There's the slightest hint of a smirk on her face as she replies, "That was the finish jump. Thank you again."

I look back. Good God, it's true. In my efforts to talk up Dusty's confidence, I walked him right past our first jump to the one next to it. The one that automatically stops the clock. We started and finished our run in the exact same second.

And it's not Dusty's fault; it's mine.

Oh, sure, most people will tell you that whatever goes wrong on the course is the handler's fault, but rarely is it so incontestably the case as it is now. People in the crowd are actually laughing at me. Several individuals come up and say, "Don't feel bad, I've done exactly the same thing." But they look like the kind of people who require spoon feeding, which sort of discounts any solace I might find in them. They might as well be chanting, "One of us! One of us!"

Fortunately, my All Fours colleagues are watching someone else's run and have thus missed this apex of ineptitude. I sit down in the empty crating area and feed Dusty half a dozen whitefish-and-potato biscuits. He's certainly earned them more than I have. After each one he licks his lips, leaving big wet smears on either side of his face. He's as thoroughly unpresentable as ever, but when I look at him I no longer see the rodentlike creature I adopted against my better judgment. What I see is a gifted athlete whose potential I unleashed and with whom I went on to win an actual agility title. That we haven't won anything since has been a persistent sore spot with me.

I consider whether I ought to set some sort of deadline—some date by which, if we're still treading water, I can just give up and get out. Retire from the game for good. Then I remember: I already *have* a deadline. When I originally undertook this endeavor, I gave myself a year. One solid year to see how far Dusty and I could go. Well, that still gives me a few months. Why not stick them out? If fate doesn't want me running agility anymore, fate can just bloody well step in and stop me.

Little do I realize I've just violated a prime rule of life which is: "Don't give fate any ideas."

CHAPTER 29

A Break in the Battle

It's my usual morning routine; I go through it almost without thought. I sling my gym bag over my shoulder and head out the back door. I open the garage, throw my bag in the car, and then double back to the yard to pick up some dog droppings I spotted en route. It just takes a few moments to scoop up the few new piles— fresh this morning, by the smell of them—then I step out to the alley to deposit them in the garbage bin. Just a small detour before I hop behind the wheel and head to my club for a workout.

The next thing I know, my leg goes out from under me and I'm hurled to the ground. As I fall, I feel a terrible shuttling of my right ankle—like a telescope closing and then opening again.

It all happened so quickly, I have to sit there, blinking, and assess what's happened. But it isn't complicated; it's an accident of the simplest kind. I command myself not to panic, even as I feel the first salvo of pain.

Fortunately, Jeffrey is working at home this morning. I take my cell phone from my jacket pocket and dial him up. "Could you meet me in the alley, please?" I ask.

"Could I— Excuse me?"

"I just slipped on a patch of ice and I can't get up."

Despite having said this, I try to rise as soon as I flip the phone shut, but my ankle won't support any weight at all, and the attempt sends electric shocks of agony up my leg. I give up and lower myself back to the concrete, and it's then that I notice that the bags of shit I've just picked up never actually made it into the trash; instead they've flown open and spatter painted me with feces. I utter a low moan of black despair.

Jeffrey appears a moment later, still pulling a fleece over his head. "I'm covered in dog crap," I tell him.

Recognizing that this is the least of my problems, he insists that we go to the hospital immediately—shit-smeared jacket and all. As I shimmy out of the way so he can pull his car out of the garage, I manage to slide myself directly through a puddle of soggy snow.

"My ass is all wet," I complain as he comes around to help me into the passenger seat.

"We'll deal with that later," he says slightly exasperated.

En route, I try to de-poo myself with the help of some paper napkins from Starbucks I have in my pocket. It's really not working. If anything, it's just grinding the mess into the fabric.

"Do you think it's broken?" he asks.

"I'm pretty sure. I think I heard it snap. With any luck I'm wrong and it's just a sprain. Is the smell bothering you? It's too cold to open a window . . ."

"Never mind the goddamn smell," he says a bit testily. I open the window anyway and toss the napkins through it. I think I read somewhere that Starbucks napkins are biodegradable. Still, I pledge to make yet another donation to Greenpeace.

Within ten minutes I'm seated in the emergency room at Swedish Covenant Hospital. Jeffrey used to work in media relations here, so he knows all the doctors. I should be in good hands. But the longer I wait, the greater the pain. In fact it becomes close to deranging, and I'm suddenly aware that I'm making rather startling noises. I can tell by the look on Jeffrey's face that he's growing increasingly alarmed, and the other people in the ER seem to inch away from me by degrees. I can't blame them; I'm the crazy, smelly, damp man who's alternately mewling like a kitten and barking like a sea lion. I might even find it funny, if my brain weren't at present trying to tear itself right out of my skull.

The ankle has swollen hideously, despite being held in by the collar of my boot. It's pretty clear that this is no mere sprain. Sprains don't induce this kind of shrieking torment. This is a fracture. Possibly a bad one.

I'm finally wheeled in to see the bone specialist—one Dr. Stamelos—who takes me in for an X-ray. "I'm going to have to hurt you," he says as I lie beneath the giant lens. I tell him he can't possibly make the pain any worse than it already is. He gives my foot a twist and I get a lesson in not saying stupid things. Later Jeffrey will tell me that my bansheelike stream of expletives (in both English and Italian) echoed down the corridor to the reception desk and caused several veteran staff members to momentarily blanch.

"Sorry," Dr. Stamelos says with an apologetic grin. "Necessary angle." Then he gives me a Vicodin and rolls me out into the hallway, where I lie abandoned on a gurney. But it's all right, the medication soon helps bring the world into some kind of rational order again, and by the time Jeffrey locates me I can breathe, even speak. Still, any hope that I might return home and continue my day as planned is pretty much dashed.

The X-ray reveals a break of sufficient seriousness to require surgery, which is booked for the day after tomorrow.

In the meantime, my leg is strapped in a splint up to the bend in my knee, and then encased in an enormous cast. As the technician applies this, he steals a glance at my X-ray and says, "You've broken this ankle before?"

"No," I say, "never."

He shrugs. "Funny, looks like it." But he's just a technician so I pay no attention.

It's only later, as I sit in the car being driven home, a new pair of crutches propped over my shoulder, that I recall I did indeed injure this very ankle when I fell on the ice up at Hounds. Oh, and prior to that, when I'd kicked that miserable rottweiler. It now seems entirely likely that I weakened the ankle in that first incident, worsened it in the second, and now, inevitably, broke it to bits this morning.

The irony is not lost on me as I hobble into the house, past my own dogs, who skitter away in fright from my clacking crutches. It will be several weeks, at least, before I'm able to walk them again. In the meantime, I'll have to hire a service to do the job for me. In attempting to protect my dogs, I've rendered myself incapable of looking after them.

I have to crawl like some kind of tree sloth up the stairs to the bedroom, where I am at last able to change out of my wet pants. I pull myself up onto the bed, position myself over the pillows, and drop onto them, utterly limp. I'd like nothing better than to nap. My body, broken and traumatized, craves it, but my mind is racing. Banking, shopping, cooking, laundry—the list of daily activities I have to desist, defer, or delegate is long and daunting. How the hell is anything going to get done if I'm not able to do it? There's also the matter of a freelance job I'm supposed to have finished by the end of the week. I've blithely procrastinated because I was confident of my ability to slam it out in just a day or two of intensive, last-minute labor. But now I've got to have surgery in two days and my schedule—not to mention my ability to think linearly on these "supersize 'em" painkillers—is up for grabs.

And then, as the icing on the cake, I recall that my next agility trial is just a little over two weeks away. I certainly won't be able to drive by then. Out of desperation I briefly consider hiring a car service. Arriving in a Saab 9-3 garners me enough dirty looks; pulling up in a Lincoln Town Car with a driver in a jacket and tie would be pushing my rep right over the edge. Plus, even if I did manage to get there, *hello*, I still wouldn't be able to *run the damn dog*.

For the fist time something like grief gets hold of me, and I have to choke back frustrated tears. Never mind the house falling apart because I can't lift a finger to maintain it; never mind going broke because I have to renege on a job at the last minute. The thing that gut punches me, emotionally, is the thought of ending Dusty's career on this frustrating, downbeat note. "So much for my vaunted ambition," I tell myself. "So much for seeing how far I could go in a year." Which is really just self-pity, and I know it. I had already accepted some time ago that Dusty and I were not cut out to go very far. Swift progress just isn't on Dusty's one-year plan.

But through the miasma of misery, I begin thinking about our last run, when I led Dusty entirely astray. He was all set to Q and I sabotaged him with my stupidity. I can't help but wonder if I'm the bad apple: what if *I've* hampered Dusty's success? What if he's stalled due to *my* limitations? That we haven't won anything in months has been a persistent sore spot with me. But I'd never considered the possibility that perhaps I've taken Dusty as far as I can. That he might be better off if I turned him over to a different handler—someone with a fresh approach, who might be able to break through the impasse I've reached with him.

I put the brakes on this increasingly self-pitying train of thought. This is all just foolish speculation. There's no guaranteeing Dusty would perform better for anyone else. In fact there's a strong case to be made against it. After all, there's his unfailing misanthropy; he flat-out refuses to warm to anyone other than Jeffrey and me. Hell, he won't even go *near* anybody but Jeffrey and me. So that settles it right there. He'll have to wait for me to recuperate.

I'm about to drop the whole matter and return to more urgent considerations when Jeffrey himself appears with a cup of hot tea, triggering an entirely new idea. "This should help you relax," he says as he places the cup on the bedside table. "Anything else I can do for you?"

"As a matter of fact," I say, my mind suddenly working furiously, "there is."

"What?" He stands upright and wipes the steam from his hands onto his jeans. "More pillows?"

"Not even close," I say, pausing theatrically for a moment. "What would you think about running Dusty at his next agility meet?"

He glances over his shoulder, like I might be talking to someone behind him. "Who, me?"

"I'll fill you in. It's not for a couple weeks. You don't have to do both days, only Sunday, if you like. I just hate for him to miss the whole weekend. We had so much momentum going after the last trial." I'm talking like a lunatic—I can see it in Jeffrey's aghast expression. But I can't stop. "There are at least two of Dee's Thursday classes before then. You can go and train in my place, get up to speed." He's looking more and more dubious, so I add, "I'll come along and give you moral support. Come on, it'll be just the *once*. How bad can it be?"

At this point Dusty bounds into the room and onto the bed, then settles down next to me and heaves a contented sigh. Jeffrey looks from him to me and says, "He's really your dog, though. Always has been."

I muse on this a bit. A working relationship between Dusty and Jeffrey might drastically alter their entire dynamic. So much so that it might supercede Dusty's and my relationship even after I'm back on my feet. The whole arc of this past year has been *my* journey with Dusty, how far *I* might take him. Now that I physically can't take him anywhere at all, I realize that I have to put aside my own ambitions and let someone else have a shot. It's high time I reminded myself that this is about Dusty, not me. And if Jeffrey can supply the spark that pushes him just that little bit further, I've got to accept that. For Dusty's sake.

"That'll change when you start working with him. You'll be

amazed. Trust me on this." I tell him about Dee and Keith—how he ran her dog when she was laid up. I decide not to say how well that worked out for them.

With the weight of precedent against him, Jeffrey can only agree—which he does monosyllabically, then shies away.

After he's gone, I lie there looking at Dusty, who's curled up asleep on the edge of the mattress. Things could indeed change when Jeffrey takes him over. But all this is useless speculation. They haven't even taken their first jump yet. Possibly they'll be a disaster together. Not that I want that—or do I? No, of course I don't. Anyway, it's silly getting all worked up about it now. Especially since I've got plenty of more immediate problems hounding me.

Like, how am I ever going to get any sleep with four pounds of masonry clamped to my leg?

CHAPTER 30

Hop Alone

The Yahoo! group, on hearing my news, immediately dubs me Hopalong. This for some strange reason gives me a swell of pride I never imagined a nickname could incite—I really feel part of this group—and I take to signing my e-mails that way.

Jason suggests I learn to stand in the middle of the ring and just point Dusty to the obstacles. He's kidding, of course; he knows full well that for Dusty pointing would be, well, pointless. Diane is closer to the mark when she suggests I get a Segway. And Dee commiserates by retelling the story of her own shattered ankle. "I broke mine on the front step to my house," she writes, "but I told people at trials it was while I was skydiving naked. It made a better story. It happened just when I was chasing Darby's MACH. Running in a cast builds character!" And in fact I do remember her teaching class while on crutches. Men may have the edge over women in sheer physical strength, but, ye gods, they beat us cold when it comes to stamina.

Since running in a cast is not something I care to consider, I try gently, and in small doses, to acquaint Jeffrey with agility's rules and conventions. It's not terribly difficult stuff, but he listens with a kind of vaporous "this isn't really happening" demeanor—as though he thinks I might in a few days toss aside my crutches, pronounce myself cured, and then go on a ten-mile jog. Or maybe it's all so simple that he's just humoring me by even appearing to listen and is counting on everything falling into place when he gets to class.

Which, admittedly, it probably will. It's canine agility, not chaos theory. What I haven't told him, he's perfectly capable of figuring out. I've just got to trust him. He's certainly earned my trust. In the days following my surgery, he's taken over running the household with such boldness and brio that I can't help feeling a little, well, irrelevant. I'd been accustomed to thinking of myself as indispensable.

And possibly I am, to Dusty. How's he going to react to having Jeffrey suddenly there giving him orders instead of me? Dogs are creatures of habit, thriving on routine. I can't imagine anything more jolting than this kind of switcheroo. The idea of him refusing to accept it, and just rebelling or falling apart, plagues me. It doesn't help that I have nothing to do but lie on my back and let my mind wander where it will.

When we arrive at Dee's class on Thursday night, I perch on my crutches outside the ring and send Jeffrey in to warm up. He unhooks Dusty and takes him over the dog walk, through the tire, over a few jumps. He looks a little stiff and uncertain at first, but as he makes his way around the room he loosens up. As for Dusty, he looks fine. Peppy, even. I know I should be relieved. But would some *token* show of unwillingness or confusion be too much to ask?

The other dogs now come spilling in for their warm-ups and Dusty grows shy and tentative. I call out to Jeffrey, "Just keep him motivated and focused on you!" and he gives me a look back that says all too clearly, "Thank you I know, and please do not narrate my evening." So I bite my tongue and try to content myself with merely observing. It's a very odd feeling, watching Dusty perform from this angle. His tail is wagging, he's smiling—obviously he's enjoying himself. Is he always like that?

After the warm-ups Dee calls the class together. She introduces Jeffrey as a guest handler, then gets down to the exercises. As usual she's laid out a few courses incorporating the various obstacles in different permutations, and everybody lines up to have a go at them.

Jeffrey does surprisingly well. Dusty stays with him, goes where he's told, and even nails a six-weave-pole set on the first try. I nearly keel over. Dee must know what I'm feeling, because she looks over at me and mouths the word, "Honeymoon." I feel immediately consoled.

Afterward Jeffrey comes over and asks, "Was that a clean run?" He's obviously already picked up the lingo. I tell him yes, it certainly was clean. "It felt clean." Okay, we can stop saying clean now.

He asks if I have any suggestions, and in fact there are a few things I've noticed. For instance, he sometimes uses the wrong arm to direct Dusty to an obstacle, which can throw the dog off (you always want to use the arm nearest to the animal). Also, his handling is just a little softer than it should be. It's like he's offering suggestions more than giving commands. But the moment I try to tell him these things, his face goes rigid, and I can tell it's too much, too fast. What he really wants to hear is how good a job he's doing. So I backpedal and tell him that, and he smiles again, rejoining the others.

I get distracted by people arriving for the advanced class. These are my usual training partners. They've all heard about my accident and want to kid me or commiserate or hear the story again from my own lips. I comply while trying to keep an eye on Jeffrey and Dusty. Each time I steal a glance I find them doing pretty well, though Jeffrey occasionally has the appearance of someone trying to carry two gallons of Jell-O in a one-gallon tub.

When the class ends, he comes out breathless and slick with sweat. "Man, that is way harder than it looks," he gasps, and I'm very gratified to hear this, though a little disturbed that he's apparently thought I've been slacking all these years. On the drive home he asks, "So am I ready for the trial?"

"I think so. You've got most of the moves down and you're functioning as a team. You could probably continue practicing, but honestly I think it's more helpful to learn by doing."

"It's mainly Dusty," he says. "For most of the class, he was the one leading *me*." And with that my singed pride is salved. I'm not entirely out of the equation; what I've taught Dusty, he's now teaching someone else.

The morning of the trial arrives. By this time my cast has come off and I've been given a big black walking boot that straps on all the way up my calf. It makes a significant difference in my quality of life—since it's removable I can once again shower and drive and sleep unencumbered—but its sole is thicker than any of the shoes

I wear on my other foot, so that while I'm able to walk and glad of it, I'm always tilting leeward and in peril of toppling over. Since toppling over is something I never want to do again, I've taken to using a cane to counterbalance. I look a bit freakish lurching around with my Frankenstein foot and wielding a cudgel, but I've been housebound so long that it'd take more than mere pride to keep me from venturing out today.

When I get downstairs, I find Jeffrey packing a cooler with a variety of sandwiches, several kinds of fruit, and assorted bags of chips and cookies. "Are we going to an agility trial?" I ask. "Or driving south to feed Katrina refugees?"

"Don't be silly," he says, shutting the lid. "Katrina was years ago." And with that he wheels the cooler outside.

I limp after him and he shuts the door behind me. Just before he locks it he says, "Can you think of anything else we need?"

I shrug. "Oh, just . . . you know. *The dog.*"

He turns the key while tossing his head over his shoulder. "He's already out."

I turn and look, and sure enough Dusty's in the yard, reclining by the fence and looking very much at ease. Why didn't I ever think of that? I've always made my preparations with Dusty inside and underfoot, so that by the time I got him out the door he was already good and rattled. I have to wonder just how much more humbling I'll have to endure before this experience is over.

Traffic is light, so we arrive at the Sportsplex in St. Charles well before noon. One of my worries is that Jeffrey won't deal well with all the downtime at the trial, that he'll get fidgety and impatient or, worse, that he'll see my All Fours colleagues as a bunch of freakish cult members. It turns out he's much more comfortable hanging around in a canvas chair than I am and falls into easy conversation with the rest of the team. It probably helps that they're doing their best to make him feel welcome and supported. Meanwhile I come in for some good-natured ribbing, because it's the first time anyone's seen me with my cane. Any hopes I'd had of coming off as Churchillian are pretty much dashed.

The facility is another indoor soccer arena that's been temporarily customized for agility. One of its courts is made over for standard, the other for jumpers. Unfortunately, our jumpers run is first. I'd have preferred that Jeffrey start with standard, which we still run in novice, but he'll have to tackle this more difficult open course instead. I go over the map with him and try not to comment on how fiendishly tough it looks. There are lots of tight corners and hairpin turns. I'd have trouble running this one myself. Eighteen obstacles in all. "Are there always this many?" Jeffrey asks, his pupils starting to dilate. Performance anxiety is grabbing hold.

I send him out for his walk-through, resisting the urge to go with him. "Let go and let God . . . ," I tell myself. Also, I'm pretty slow on my feet these days and I don't want to hold him back. But when Betsy kindly volunteers to go out and help him, I find myself unable to sit idly by; even if I can't keep up, joining him will be easier on me than anxiously craning my neck to watch him from the sidelines.

I reach him moments after Betsy does. He's just started showing her the attack he's got planned. I stick my head in between theirs, and as I do my clumsy boot propels me forward a bit too swiftly, so that I come across as much more of a busybody than I really intended. Jeffrey and Betsy exchange a glance—oh, fine,

I've given them cause to form a bond against me!—then Jeffrey resumes sketching out his course for us.

He actually has a pretty good idea of what he needs to do and how to do it; though when I originally explained the concept of turning to get your dog on your opposite side without losing momentum, I apparently neglected to tell him the correct term for it (which is *front cross*) because he now announces that, on the far side of a certain jump, he'll be doing a "pirouette." Betsy finds this so cute she can hardly stand it. Jeffrey's cheeks flush hot pink with embarrassment, and I quietly shrink back, hoping he has a good run so he forgets to give me hell for this afterward.

The competition begins with the big dogs. Jeffrey watches each team to pick up pointers on what they do right and, almost more valuably, how they screw up. He's taking this very seriously, which is gratifying; I couldn't have borne it if he'd treated it as some kind of lark, free of consequences. But then I should've known better. He's always had a keen competitive streak. In fact he's got himself so geared up that I feel compelled to put the brakes on his ambition a bit. "Just remember," I tell him, "there's no expectation here. It's your first run ever, it's in open instead of novice, and the course is a tough one. Just concentrate on getting through it."

"Screw that," he says. "We're gonna tear the place down."

I just smile and nod, because it's not my job to humble him. That's Dusty's. And of course he does exactly that. He refuses to jump, runs circles around the weave poles, and pops out of the tunnel from the same side he entered it. He's really giving Jeffrey a crash course in "*La la la la la*, I can't hear you."

Jeffrey looks absolutely stricken afterward, so much so that all his annoyance with me is utterly forgotten. "What went wrong?" he asks as he mops his face with his discarded sweatshirt.

I can only shrug. "If I knew that, I'd have had him running in excellent by now. Sometimes he's just not with you."

He plops down into his chair. "How much water did I bring?"

I open the cooler and root through it. "Four bottles."

"I'll take two of them now."

The novice standard run is a fairly straightforward course compared to the one Jeffrey barely survived earlier, although it does have the disadvantage of featuring the full complement of obstacles. There's even a set of broad jumps thrown in. But he walks it several times (this time without my help), and he's so far recovered from his earlier calamity that he's back to feeling confident—even cocky. He hands me his video cam and asks me to record the run.

"Are you sure?" I say.

He half smirks, as if to say, "Dude. Please."

And—what do you know. He lines Dusty up, and when the timekeeper says go they sail right over the first jump, and the momentum from that carries them clear up the A-frame, like the breath of God is puffing away at Dusty's tail. From there Jeffrey pulls one his "pirouettes" to get Dusty into the tunnel, and while it doesn't quite work as planned, somehow Dusty figures out where he's meant to go, and goes there—it's almost like he and Jeffrey are compensating for each other's lapses.

And that's when I start watching him, in a way I'm never able to when I'm running beside him. And yes it's true he's not a fast dog, nor is he poetry in motion or an unstoppable juggernaut or

anything like that. He's a little wad of scruff with a scrap of determination, that's all. But there are times—when he's right at the
apex of a jump, with his forelegs stretched before him and his hind
feet still recoiling from the launch; or when he's plunging through
the tire, the velocity streaking the fur on his face and splaying his
cheeks into a smile; or when he's loping across the dog walk, his
head low and his tail erect—that he seems suddenly beautiful,
suddenly graceful, suddenly powerful. They're just split-second
images, flashes, nothing more, but they have the startling effect of
drop-kicking me into profound emotion. In this setting, I'm seeing him for the first time as separate from me—not just physically, in the sense that I'm not out there with him, but as an
entirely separate entity. And it occurs to me that I really do love
the little guy. For all his peculiarities and pathologies, he has such
tremendous dignity. The blood of wolves runs in his veins, the
race memory of primeval packs that took down mastodons, the
pedigree of canine legions who sprinted alongside the armies of
Alexander. I can see all this in him, and I'm aware as never before
that as fiercely loyal as he may be, he doesn't disappear when I'm
not there. In fact outside my shadow he seems to grow larger—as
does his integrity, his *honor*.

I've just begun humming "Summon the Heroes" when he and
Jeffrey reach the teeter and everything comes apart at the seams.
Once again he's a nineteen-pound head case dithering wildly on a
glorified playground.

But I can't forget what I've just glimpsed in him. Afterward I
play back the video of the run, trying to recapture the sensation,
but the camera is small and Dusty is barely visible—just a little
charcoal blip moving across the puny screen. Never mind, it's all

still in my head, etched indelibly on my brain. I've seen my dog in an entirely new light—seen him as something *besides* my dog—something greater and grander. What this means for our relationship, I'm still too shaken to know or guess.

On the drive home, Jeffrey asks, "Do you have any suggestions on how I might improve?"

"What?" I say, certain I can't have heard him correctly. " 'Improve'? You—you actually want to do this *again*?"

"Sure!" He turns and calls over his shoulder, "We've got to win, right Dusty? *Win win win!*"

What have I set in motion here? I've effectively cut myself out of my own projected destiny. My dog, my partner—both are rushing off to glory on their own, leaving me behind, choking on their dust. The world has gone topsy-turvy. There's a weight bearing down on me, the sky above us is big and heavy, and so is my leg. I lean back in my seat and close my eyes, and try not to think about it.

Terry Simons is on TV again, standing with someone who's smiling just as hard as he is. And I know who it is, I *do*:

> TERRY: I'M HERE WITH JEFFREY SMITH, OUR SIXTEEN-INCH WINNER! JEFFREY, WHAT'S THE SECRET TO YOUR SUCCESS?
> JEFFREY: I have to thank my partner, Rob, who did a lot of preliminary work with Dusty before I took over and made him a champion.

TERRY: IS YOUR PARTNER HERE TONIGHT?
JEFFREY: No Terry, he's at home with a broken
ankle that refuses to heal. Medical science is baffled
by his condition . . .

I'm jolted awake by a speed bump. I blink and look out the window; we're cruising down our street.

As I hobble into the house, Carmen's there to greet me—no, not me—she's looking past me. Everybody's looking past me these days.

I wander upstairs to revel in self-pity, shutting the door and taking some extra shut-eye. When I'm finally sufficiently rested, I yawn, stretch, and stumble across the hallway to check my e-mail. There's already a message from Jeffrey:

> I took the liberty of checking your calendar. I have nothing scheduled April 19–20 and would relish the opportunity to QQ if you are still hobbled. I will work on my pirouette technique, as it does not appear all that seamless on the video.
>
> It was great bonding with Dusty today; he seems to look at me differently, like he's the Karate Kid and I'm Al Morita. Thank you for trusting me with his handling.

At this point, there's really nothing for me to do but give in.

CHAPTER 31

At the Crossroads

Weeks pass. I'm able to dispense with the cane, but the boot remains for the foreseeable future, which of course means I'm unable to run Dusty when April 19 rolls around. Just as well, 'cause if I were, I'd have a struggle on my hands wrenching him back from Jeffrey. He's been looking forward to this with a kind of crazy confidence that alarms me. He's obsessed with qualifying—and since that's really another way of saying "glory," I can't really criticize. The difference is that I gave myself a year. Jeffrey's done exactly two runs to date and feels he's overdue. He expects to end this weekend bedecked with blue ribbons and smiles all around. Failure, as Mrs. Thatcher once pronounced from a slightly more enviable perch, is not an option.

Upon our arrival, Jeffrey nearly sprints onto the court, map in hand, and starts strutting like the cock of the walk. Meantime I set up Dusty's crate and our chairs and greet the other All Fours attendees—Marilyn, Diane, Alise, and Cyndi, so far, with several others expected as the days draws on. They're all friendly enough, but their eyes keep straying to Jeffrey. Something about him intrigues them; possibly it's his shimmering positivity and beguiling naïveté. They all seem to want to tweak his cheek and stroke his mop of hair. I'm not jealous, though. I'm *not*.

Once Dusty's secure in his crate and has ample water in his dish, I thump out to see what Jeffrey's come up with. It's a fairly straightforward course. The first third is easily handled with the dog on the left, then there's a middle section where it's best to switch to the right before going back to the left for the finish. So there are only three places Jeffrey needs to front cross—or pirouette, as we now refer to it, completely unironically. Simple stuff.

But he has a question. "When I pirouette," he says, "do I go clockwise or counterclockwise?"

I blink. "Well, that depends what side you're . . . Look, you don't really need to think that way. It's just a matter of switching sides while keeping the dog in your line of sight. Here," I say, and I demonstrate pretending to come off a jump, extending my left arm to focus the hypothetical dog's attention, then swiftly replacing it with my right as I pivot myself to his other flank.

Jeffrey nods and says, "So . . . that's counterclockwise."

"Yes, but that's irreleva—" A whistle blows; it's time for the judge's briefing. I hobble off the course and let Jeffrey join his fellow handlers. In fact this spurt of activity has taken its toll on me, and I have to go plop myself down in my chair for a while, remove the boot, and massage my ankle. I'm feeling better by the time competition begins, so I strap my leg back in and go off in search of Jeffrey.

I find him at a small cafeteria table overlooking the ring, the course map spread out before him. He's drawing little circles where he means to front cross, with arrows to indicate the direction, clockwise or counterclockwise.

"You're making this a lot harder than it needs to be," I tell him.

He looks up at me with threatening blankness and says, "Would you just give me a moment here, please?"

Hooo-*kay*. I back off and head back down to the crating area, where I sit down among the others. After a while the conversation turns to television. "You know," someone says, "I was watching my favorite show last night, *What Not to Wear*. You ever see that?" Several of us nod. "I just love it. Anyway, it occurred to me that everyone in this entire place—me included—could easily be on that show." She pauses as Jeffrey arrives on the scene, then adds, "Well . . . not Jeff." It's true: alone on this vast sartorial crime scene, he's perfectly fitted out in designer jeans, a peach polo shirt with plaid trim along the inside collar, and laceless sneakers. He's A&F; everyone else is 4-H.

As it happens, his run is quite respectable but not the stuff blue ribbons are made of. Everything goes well except the weaves; Dusty pops out after the third pole, and try though he might Jeffrey can't get him back in correctly. He keeps gesturing and calling and following Dusty around, while Dusty goes in circles, not comprehending a thing. I actually feel sorry for him. He looks like he's trying desperately to swat a giant fly.

Eventually, he gives up on the weaves and calls Dusty to finish the run. That works better, but he looks crestfallen when he rejoins me. "You have to complete the weaves to qualify, right?" he asks, even though he knows the answer.

"Afraid so," I say. He scowls as his last hope of a double-Q weekend evaporates. "But listen, it was a very good run, everything else was spot on."

"I know, I know," he says, and he squats down to give Dusty some congratulatory manhandling. "You did great, boy! And next time we're gonna come in first!"

Gotta give the man props for elasticity. He's bounced back faster than I ever did. Any faster and he'd risk whiplash.

But then, the ensuing hours make it clear that Jeffrey's more suited to just about *everything* in these environs than I am. I'd worried about him growing restive during the hours of downtime, but it turns out he's not one to take a little thing like having nothing to do get in the way of his fun. After the jumpers course is rebuilt for novice, Jeffrey volunteers to be a bar setter, which involves sitting on the course during the competition and running out to replace any bars that get knocked loose. I never thought of doing that. He looks very alert and engaged out there, and is Johnny-on-the-spot whenever one of the novice dogs blasts through the bar jumps like they were Tinkertoys. Later, when the novice class ends and he's relieved of his duties, he comes back smiling and fresh faced and boasting of having learned a lot by watching the handlers and dogs up close. An hour or so later he reappears with a limp paper plate bearing a soggy sloppy joe; turns out all volunteers are treated to a free lunch. Which to Jeffrey appears quite a deal; he bites into the molten mass with gusto. Some of its aroma wafts my way and burns my eyes.

The next time I see him, he's clutching a chain of perforated red tickets; he's spent thirty dollars entering the prize drawing. "What prize drawing?" I ask. He jerks his thumb toward the standard ring, and I limp on over to check it out. Sure enough, it's there big as life: a table filled with dog-related prizes that are being raffled off, including an enormous pooper-scooper kit that comes with a rake and silver trash can affixed to a platform with wheels. People are oohing and aahing over it. I must have passed this display a dozen times this morning, as I went back and forth between standard and jumpers to watch my teammates run their dogs, and I never even noticed it.

After a midafternoon snack—fresh fruit and savory biscuits, packed of course by Jeffrey—I announce that I'm feeling a little tired.

"Take a nap," says Jeffrey.

I shake my head. "Impossible. I can't sleep at trials. I've tried, believe me. Every time I close my eyes my hearing becomes, like, Kryptonian. I just can't tune anything out."

He deftly produces his iPod, which is already set to some soothing New Agey compositions by Jean-Michel Jarre. I plug in the earbuds and lower my lids and the world disappears. Within minutes I'm pulled bodily into the arms of Morpheus. My last conscious thought is of Jeffrey, and how I may have to kill him and dispose of his body to restore my withering self-confidence.

My self-esteem isn't much bolstered when, after awakening from my snooze, I'm told—by Marilyn, by Dee, by Besty, by *everybody*—that "you're not getting Dusty back." Jeffrey's energy, his keenness, his commitment (he's already subscribed to *Clean Run* magazine, something I never quite got around to doing in six years), along with his charm, wit, and good looks, have all combined to push me definitively to the sidelines. He even wins the goddamn raffle, and is soon loading the giant pooper-scooper kit into his convertible.

The only discordant note is his actual performance. He and

Dusty haven't quite meshed as a team, and there are no qualifying scores, much less blue ribbons. Even so, I can see him improving as he goes, mastering the learning curve even as it steepens before him. He's intelligent, ambitious, and quite shockingly gung ho.

As for me, I'm relegated to support staff. It's my job to do things like take videos of his runs so that he can put them on You-Tube for the benefit of posterity.

And in fact it's in this capacity that something unexpected befalls me. It's the last run of the weekend, late Sunday afternoon. Novice standard. Jeffrey's last chance to qualify. I'm positioned outside the ring, video cam in hand, as he and Dusty head to the line. Because the ring is normally used as a soccer field, there's a high Plexiglas shield around it, and I'm having trouble aiming the camcorder through the glare. When Jeffrey starts the run, I edge around the perimeter toward the center of the course where the light isn't so intrusive.

And that's when it happens. Dusty comes out of a tunnel facing me and his eyes lock onto mine. It's only a split-second thing, but in that instant our old rapport comes barreling back—that indelible, empathic bond built up over months and months of training and teamwork—and I can almost hear him thinking, "What are you doing out there? You're supposed to be in here!"

And then he starts trotting toward me.

Behind him, Jeffrey howls, "Dusty! Dusty, *come!*" but Dusty ignores him utterly. He's headed my way, smiling ear to ear.

I realize this is a crisis, but for a moment I'm frozen. I have no idea how to react. Finally, desperately, I just drop to my knees and hide. I cower there, almost not daring to breathe, listening as

Jeffrey's shouts become more and more insistent. After a few seconds I peer up over the partition, just in time to see Dusty casually exiting the field, presumably to look for me, and leaving Jeffrey behind to stew in righteous frustration.

There's no point in hiding any longer, so I get to my feet and go to face the music, knowing the tune's not going to be a pleasant one. All I can say in my defense is that I had no idea my presence would prove so fatally distracting.

I find Jeffrey just outside the finish gate. He's managed to catch up with Dusty and leash him and is now commiserating with Marilyn, who is absolutely furious on his behalf. As soon as I catch her eye I shake my head and poke my finger to my chest, to signal that, "Yes, it was my fault. I know. Mea culpa, mea culpa, mea maxima bloody culpa."

It probably doesn't help that Dusty happily leaps up on me when I reach him. I can't help it, and so I capitulate, caressing his head. As bad as this all has been, and as angry as I'm sure Jeffrey is, it's still kind of flattering. I'd been disappointed by the ease with which Jeffrey had replaced me as Dusty's handler, and till now Dusty hadn't shown even a glimmer of confusion or displeasure.

Now that he has—in the most disgraceful way and at the most inopportune moment imaginable—my pride is salved. But it leaves me with a whole new dilemma. All weekend long I've complained about being sidelined. Now it seems even the sidelines are off limits.

I have only two choices: to step back into the ring and resume complete control of Dusty, or to hand him over to Jeffrey for good.

Realistically, it'll be several weeks before I'm healed enough to do the former, and even if were just a matter of days, I don't know if I'd have the heart. When I asked Jeffrey to fill in for me, I never dreamed I'd be launching him onto a lifelong pursuit.

I started down this path looking for glory, and I think I just may find it. Albeit, not in any way I ever anticipated. Never mind: reflected glory is still glory.

And maybe, just maybe, it's the best possible kind.

EPILOGUE

Never Give Up

After I retire myself from Dusty's handling, something in me relaxes. I feel a kind of spiritual unclenching. It's tremendously liberating to have no more agenda, to be free from the constant rounds of training and competing, to wake up on a Saturday morning with the weekend ahead of me, wide open and unstructured, just waiting to be lived moment by moment, to no longer have to drive to Plano or Spring Grove, or to Dogpatch or Hooterville or anyplace at all.

And yet—as time passes I start to itch (and not on my ankle, which is now restored to reasonable soundness). It's just that whenever Jeffrey returns home from a trial, brimming with stories (and an occasional ribbon), I can't help feeling a twinge of envy. I find myself thinking back fondly on the days when I thought Dusty and I might go the distance. Be the best of the best. Be *champions*.

And then one day I realize that dream isn't necessarily lost to me. All I need is . . .

I start surfing the rescue society Web sites—collies this time. Quite a few of the big, beautiful boys and girls they have up for adoption look very promising. Then I come upon the photo of a lean-looking sable who, even in repose, gives off a definite whiff of crazy. The text below the picture reads:

> Hi, my name is Harley and this is my second time through Collie Rescue. I was first given up because my original owner's son had moved back home and had allergies. I was very spoiled and had been allowed to do anything I wanted. I was adopted out but proved a bit much for an inexperienced owner to handle, as Collie Rescue found out when I was returned. I have very high herding instincts and drive and will not be happy to be just a pet. I need a person who's interested in a dog to have fun with in agility, obedience, fly ball, or herding—I need something to do; I need a job. I get along with other dogs and cats and ride well in a car. I am also crate trained and housebroken. I do need a fenced yard and should add that I am very vocal when I'm out in it! I'm looking for someone who has a lot of dog sense and a strong personality and can prove they can train a dog successfully. I will need to continue my obedience classes so whoever adopts me must be willing to register for these. I am very intelligent and ready to learn but need someone to help me. Only serious inquiries please. Thanks, Harley.

There are more red flags here than in a May Day parade in Beijing. Even so, my writer's mind starts taking the expected turn. Perhaps this Harley is a nascent agility genius who merely needs encouragement and a firm hand to draw out his talents. "No no," I tell myself, "that way lies madness." And I sit down to e-mail an enquiry about one of the gorgeous tricolors with chipper mugs and clear, bright eyes whose glowing testimonials contain no hint of latent psychosis.

But it's like my hands are on autopilot. My fingers move independently across the keyboard, composing, as I suppose I always knew they must:

"Hello, I would like to adopt Harley . . ."

ACKNOWLEDGMENTS

Deepest thanks to Haven Kimmel, whose dog sense is more acute than that of anyone else I know, and whose encouragement and generosity were invaluable to me during the writing of this book.

Thanks to my agent, Christopher Schelling, who nudged me for two years to undertake this project; he is the wisest man I know, and possibly the prettiest.

Thanks to my editor, Luke Dempsey, who had faith in this endeavor, and who taught me a thing or two about caustic wit.

Thanks to Augusten Burroughs for his support and friendship, and for his superb example as a memoirist and essayist.

Thanks to Scott Browning and the staff of Hall Farm Center for the Arts, whose residency program allowed me the time and space to write the initial chapters of this narrative.

If anyone was essential to this story, it's the singular Dee Corboy-Lulik, a visionary trainer and an inspirational coach; all her students adore her with equal fervor, I'm just the only one to write a book about it. So far.

Acknowledgments

Thanks to the members of the All-Fours Agility team for teaching me the true meaning of community, chiefly Andi Skillman, Marilyn Paker, Cyndi Gibson, Debbie Sazma, Gus Pusateri, Carl and Kim Hibben, Kevin and Elysee Quealy, Deb Konrath, Alise Carrico, Jason Libasci, Diane Dillon, Sue Bowman, Betsy Easton, Eryn Paker, Cindy Aldridge, Sharon O'Connell, and Stacy Nigrelli.

I must also pay tribute to the dogs who left us during the writing of this book: Deb's beautiful Brittany, Sue's irrepressible Spencer, and Andi's sweet Whisper. They will all be missed.

Thanks to Sally Alatallo for recommending agility to me in the first place.

Thanks to Natalie Whalen and the Central Illinois Sheltie Rescue for all the good work they do, and especially for placing Dusty with me.

Thanks to Annie Morse and Kevin Pierce for their Attic wit, inimitable hospitality, and priceless friendship.

Eternal gratitude to Bunny Boyt and my other neighbors who are paragons of patience and forbearance.

Enduring thanks and love to Jeffrey Smith for stepping in to save the day when it really needed saving—which is pretty much what he does for me every day.

And finally, thanks to Carmen, Dusty, and Harley. Here words are insufficient, and they wouldn't understand them anyway.

About the Author

Robert Rodi is the owner of three dogs and the author of seven novels. He's also written short stories, literary criticism, and works for the stage. He divides his time between Chicago, where he was born, and Siena, Italy. In dog years he is 350.